Praise for *Solution-Focused RTI*

"This is a remarkably refreshing approach to Response to Intervention. Metcalf offers a clear, jargon-free perspective that focuses on identifying and building on the strengths of students through collaborative conversations and interventions that offer solutions and, ultimately, the best chance of success. *Solution-Focused RTI* is not simply a book of ideas. It is chock full of clear illustrations, real-world vignettes, and examples of school-based interventions that are applicable to *all* students."

—Bob Bertolino, Ph.D., associate professor,
Rehabilitation Counseling, Maryille University,
senior clinical advisor, Youth in Need, Inc.

"I would buy this book immediately and find it of inestimable value in my work. I would also give a copy to every ESE specialist, principal, and guidance counselor I know. *Solution-Focused RTI* takes a fresh and novel approach that will give hope in hopeless situations—and that is exactly what we need right now."

—Anne Rambo, Ph.D., associate professor,
Nova Southeastern University

"This book provides perspectives and examples of how to positively motivate students by applying solution-focused principles to the school setting."

—Gerald Corey, Ed.D., professor emeritus,
California State University, Fullerton

"Linda Metcalf hits upon the single-most important element typically missing from the RTI discussion: the power of capitalizing on strengths rather than student problems. This is a life-altering read for teachers, administrators, and school counselors who are seeking a positive approach to student success. It provides highly successful—and doable—intervention strategies to use with even the most challenging situations.

"Metcalf describes actual elementary, middle, and high-school situations drawing together the latest research and practice from RTI and solution-focused strategies, showing how teachers, administrators, and school counselors can collaborate to make classrooms places of joy, purpose, caring, and collaboration."

—Loretta Whitson, executive director,
California School Counselors Association

Jossey-Bass Teacher

Jossey-Bass Teacher provides educators with practical knowledge and tools to create a positive and lifelong impact on student learning. We offer classroom-tested and research-based teaching resources for a variety of grade levels and subject areas. Whether you are an aspiring, new, or veteran teacher, we want to help you make every teaching day your best.

From ready-to-use classroom activities to the latest teaching framework, our value-packed books provide insightful, practical, and comprehensive materials on the topics that matter most to K–12 teachers. We hope to become your trusted source for the best ideas from the most experienced and respected experts in the field.

Solution-Focused RTI

A Positive and Personalized Approach to Response to Intervention

Linda Metcalf

JOSSEY-BASS
A Wiley Imprint
www.josseybass.com

Published by Jossey-Bass
A Wiley Imprint
989 Market Street, San Francisco, CA 94103-1741   www.josseybass.com

Jossey-Bass books and products are available through most bookstores. To contact Jossey-Bass directly call our Customer Care Department within the U.S. at 800-956-7739, outside the U.S. at 317-572-3986, or fax 317-572-4002.

Jossey-Bass also publishes its books in a variety of electronic formats. Some content that appears in print may not be available in electronic books.

Library of Congress Cataloging-in-Publication Data
Metcalf, Linda.
     Solution-focused RTI : a positive and personalized approach to response to intervention /
     Linda Metcalf.—1st ed.
          p.   cm.
     Includes bibliographical references and index.
     ISBN 978-0-470-47042-8 (pbk.)
          1. Learning disabled children—Identification.   2. Learning disabilities—Diagnosis.   3. Slow learning children—Education.   4. Action research in education.   I. Title.
     LB1029.R4M47 2010
     371.9′043—dc22

                                                                              2010000723

Printed in the United States of America
FIRST EDITION
PB Printing   10 9 8 7 6 5 4 3 2 1

About This Book

One evening in the school counseling practicum that I teach, the discussion turned to Response to Intervention (RTI). I heard groans, complaints, and frustrations and thought, "What an opportunity for solutions!" Instead of encouraging commiseration, I asked my future school counselors to describe a better way to implement RTI, using a solution-focused approach. They quickly provided this description:

- The process would be more optimistic.

- There would be less paperwork.

- There would be more involvement with parents and students.

- There would be less pressure on the teacher to be the sole source of ideas for interventions.

- The conversations would be more hopeful in that participants would leave the meeting with additional strategies for everyone.

The more we talked, the more excited I became about developing these ideas. Surely a more straightforward way of implementing Response to Intervention, based on students' strengths, could do a world of good for students and educators alike. I had created a similar program for low-achieving students in Davenport, Iowa, several years earlier; why not incorporate those ideas and my students' ideas and see what would happen? The results are laid out in this book.

If you are a teacher, administrator, or school counselor, this book will improve your Response to Intervention by helping you

- Engage students and parents in a process that is respectful, collaborative, and hopeful

- Decrease paperwork so that teachers are willing to develop interventions and track success

- Increase morale among teachers through teamwork rather than solitary strategizing

- Motivate students by enlisting their ideas when strategizing about interventions

- Involve parents by making them experts on their own child

RTI doesn't have to be met with groans anymore. Instead, it can be a collaboration between teachers, parents, and students, identifying what has worked, how it worked, and what to do to achieve success—all in a timely, effective, and hopeful manner.

About the Author

Linda Metcalf, Ph.D., is a former middle school teacher, a certified school counselor, a licensed professional counselor, and a licensed marriage and family therapist in the State of Texas. She is professor and director of school counseling at Texas Wesleyan University, where she has developed a solution-focused school counseling program for graduate students. Metcalf is an international presenter who has taught the solution-focused approach to many educators across the United States and in Canada, Japan, Singapore, Australia, Norway, Scotland, the Netherlands, England, and Germany. For five years, she consulted with Davenport Community Schools in Iowa to develop a program for challenged students facing referral for special education. The development of that program led to a new solution-focused approach to Response to Intervention. Metcalf has presented her work on solution-focused RTI to school districts across the United States.

The author of numerous professional articles, Metcalf has written many books for educators, counselors, and parents. Her other books include *Teaching Toward Solutions*, *Parenting Toward Solutions*, *Solution-Focused Group Therapy*, *A Practical Approach to Learning Family Therapy*, and her best-selling book *Counseling Toward Solutions: A Practical Solution-Focused Program for Working with Students, Teachers, and Parents*.

Dr. Metcalf is available to train your school or district staff through her "Solution-Focused RTI" workshops or for personal on-site consulting. Her workshops—which range from three-hour sessions to one- or two-day trainings—are interactive, involving brief lectures, many exercises for skill building, role plays, and video clips. She has successfully consulted with many schools to help educators implement the solution-focused approach and lower special education referrals. To learn more, call (817) 690-2229 or go to MetcalfConsulting.org.

Also by Linda Metcalf

Counseling Toward Solutions: A Practical Solution-Focused Program for Working with Students, Teachers, and Parents

The Field Guide to Counseling Toward Solutions: The Solution-Focused School

Solution-Focused Group Therapy: Ideas for Groups in Private Practice, Schools, Agencies, and Treatment Programs

Teaching Toward Solutions: A Solution-Focused Guide to Improving Student Behavior, Grades, Parental Support and Staff Morale

How to Say It to Get into the College of Your Choice: Application, Essay, and Interview Strategies to Get You the Big Envelope

Parenting Toward Solutions: How Parents Can Use Skills They Already Have to Raise Responsible, Loving Kids

The Miracle Question: Answer It and Change Your Life

The Art of Solution-Focused Therapy (with Elliott Connie)

A Practical Approach to Learning Family Therapy

Acknowledgments

It takes more than just one person to write a book. I consider myself a fortunate author to have engaged people whom I respect so much while composing this manuscript. I appreciate Marjorie McAneny at Jossey-Bass/John Wiley for her belief in this project and her patience with me in writing it. You are a delightful editor to work with. I thank Julia Parmer for her help in gathering the reviews that helped to make the book more useful. I also offer my thanks to Betty Long of Davenport Community Schools for allowing me to use the project that we developed collaboratively. Davenport will always hold a special place in my heart as a community where students are first. It was an honor to be part of your work.

I appreciate the many e-mails I have received from school counselors who listened to my ideas for solution-focused Response to Intervention in workshops through Texas Counseling Association, American Counseling Association, and American School Counseling Association conferences across the country. Your response to my interventions made me try even harder to produce a book that would make your work easier. I appreciate my many school counselor students at Texas Wesleyan University, who gave me their thoughts, complaints, and dreams for Response to Intervention. As always, I learn from you each time I teach a class. Thank you, Chris Iveson of BRIEF Therapy Practice in London; you excited my students and invigorated my thinking in regard to school strategies. When I took my students to hear you in the summer of 2009, I learned about the eBay exercise that I included in Chapters Four and Twelve of this book from you. You made learning fun and were inspirational to all of us.

Thank you, Sarah Switzer, Patti Gatlin, and Cassie Reid, extraordinary school counselors who "get it." Your work inspires me each time we talk! Sarah, you were so eager to share your stories, poem, and worksheet. Your students are fortunate. Patti, from the beginning of our friendship, your laugh and smile were contagious! How fortunate your principal and staff are to have someone with such sincerity and strong leadership skills. Cassie, as my former student, I knew from the first time I heard you reminisce about a student that I wanted your cases in this book. Thank you for taking the time during your doctoral work to produce another paper!

Finally, I thank my family, who diligently supports "one more book" project and always takes the time to ask how things are progressing. I appreciate Roger, who keeps reminding me to save my text in *at least* two places. I appreciate your support more than you realize. And Rex 1 and Rex 2, my now older golden retrievers, thanks for the walks that churned up still more ideas that ended up on these pages. We wrote another book together.

Contents

TIER II
TARGETED INSTRUCTIONAL INTERVENTIONS

TIER III
INTENSIVE INDIVIDUALIZED INTERVENTIONS

This book is dedicated to
my husband, Roger,
and my children, Ryan, Kelli, and Roger Jr.
You inspire me to always do more.
It is also dedicated to my students at Texas Wesleyan
University.
You bring new ideas and passion to your work every day!
I am proud to be your teacher.
To students with challenges,
this book is for you.
May you teach your teachers what you need.

Introduction

Year after year, students are directed by well-intentioned teachers, school counselors, school psychologists, and administrators, who are mandated by their districts to guide students with learning and behavioral challenges in a process called Response to Intervention (RTI). Those professionals spend hours trying to plan and assess strategies to help challenged students be more successful. When such good efforts fail, a student is looked at as disabled, or unable to function in a regular classroom. This approach treats students like malfunctioning ATM machines that reject the educational deposits that are put into them. Perhaps it is not the machine that is the problem; perhaps it is the manner in which the deposits are being made.

One criticism of the RTI method that is often heard suggests that RTI is really a means of limiting access to special education services. The Wikipedia entry for RTI (http://en.wikipedia.org/wiki/Response_to_intervention) says,

> The intervention model puts the focus on individual teachers to prove that they have done everything possible in the classroom before the child can be assessed. Because the RTI model is often implemented across years, assessment and classification of a student can be unreasonably delayed or never provided when each new year the student has a new teacher and a new RTI. Critics charge that requiring an extensive and lengthy paper trail prior to evaluation of a child is primarily used as a bureaucratic means for delaying that evaluation. They point to the fact that the cost of special education services is a powerful incentive for districts to systematically delay services to as many children as possible as long as possible.

It is unfortunate that such interventions are sometimes attempted only as a means to either keep students out of special education (to save funding) or get students *into* special education when teachers feel challenged by their learning differences. The purpose of the process is confusing to all. RTI was never intended to keep students out of special education. It was intended as a means of finding interventions that work for *all* students and to get them the help they need as soon as possible, when they first start showing signs of struggle in the classroom.

So how can the process developed through RTI serve as a means to discover how students learn best? What if parents and students were more involved in the process, so that everyone was working together to direct educational solutions?

What if interventions were constructed on the basis of what works for the student rather than what is not working?

The title of this book, *Solution-Focused RTI*, suggests that the process seeks solutions, yet not all RTI processes reach solutions. Currently, most RTI paperwork is overabundant and cumbersome, and the referral process centers on problems. Of course, problem identification is necessary, given that a problem is what instigates a referral, but often, meetings examine the problem more closely, looking for diagnoses, symptoms, family issues, learning disabilities, and more. Soon, the issue at hand sounds impossible, so of course the student must be referred to special education because a general education teacher can't possibly help with all of that!

So what is the solution-focused approach? It is an approach that came from the counseling profession. Yvonne Dolan, director of the Institute for Solution-Focused Therapy, explains: "As the name suggests, [Solution-Focused Brief Therapy] is future-focused, goal-directed, and focuses on solutions, rather than on the problems that brought clients to seek therapy. . . . The SFBT approach assumes that all clients have some knowledge of what would make their life better, even though they may need some (at times, considerable) help describing the details of their better life[,] and that everyone who seeks help already possesses at least the minimal skills necessary to create solutions" (http://www.solutionfocused .net/solutionfocusedtherapy.html).

The solution-focused RTI process is different from other RTI approaches in that it recognizes the existence of a problem and then identifies times when the problem is less of a problem using a team approach. Students and parents serve as consultants by remembering times when school was slightly more successful, resulting in a richer dialogue for the student. As a result, more students are able to remain in the least restricted environment (LRE). Additionally, with student and parent consultation, teachers are able to match their suggestions with research-based interventions. As a result, teachers begin to widen their beliefs about being able to teach for a wide variety of learning styles in the same classroom and parents feel more involved in the process.

Since passage of the Individuals with Disabilities Education Act (IDEA), children are not to be allowed to lag in any facet of their education, yet too often, students with unusual learning needs are placed in special education, perhaps before they should be. This book will show how children and adolescents can teach us what they need to be successful. It will show how teams of teachers, along with parents, can create opportunities for success by watching out for times when such students are slightly more successful rather than times when they are unsuccessful. This approach goes beyond taking a positive approach to education. The educator who uses the ideas in this book will become much more than positive; she will be able to see past problems, toward solutions with *every* student in her classroom. The educator will become solution focused, not problem focused.

Using this book, including its templates for Tier I, II, and III interventions, many teachers will be able to help students improve their grades and change their behavior. Parents will feel more welcome and appreciated, resulting in more school involvement on their part. Administrators will be able to spend their time on creating better programs or curricula because they will have fewer disciplinary issues to attend to and more time to spend on making schools safe and orderly. Special education referrals will decrease because more students will be able to learn in regular classrooms, leaving more time and space for children who truly need the additional resources of special education.

This book is divided into three sections, based on the three tiers of Response to Intervention. Each chapter will provide information, applications, and case studies to pique the reader's interest and offer inspiration. Appendix A provides reproducible copies of the forms and Appendix B is a list of Internet resources. This book is written for all educators: classroom teachers who are asked to create interventions to help students be more successful; administrators who are asked by their school district to provide an RTI program in their schools; and school counselors, school psychologists, and social workers who are often called on to begin, implement, and participate in the RTI process.

The time is ripe for a more collaborative kind of RTI in which school counselors, school psychologists, teachers, and administrators—*along with students and parents*—work together on the process. No longer should a teacher sit alone in a classroom, seeking ideas for RTI and filling out numerous forms to describe attempts to help his student. Instead, he can step outside the traditional RTI team setting and put questions about interventions into the hands of students, colleagues, and parents, resulting in better relationships, more buy-in, and more motivation.

So consider this possibility: Every student, parent, teacher, principal, school counselor, and staff member in your school already possesses the skills to create solutions that will help students be successful.

Wow. You have been working way too hard! You've got experts all over your classroom and all over your school. How will you begin to mine such resources? Read on.

Solution-Focused RTI

Tier I

Core Instruction for All Students

The Response-to-Intervention process consists of three tiers. Tier I policies suggest that all learners have the right to the best possible learning environment, which optimizes their chances of academic success and behavioral success. The chapters on Tier I present useful solution-focused strategies that teachers have successfully implemented in order to address behavioral and academic issues. The teachers who are described are good examples of how to meet the Tier I expectation of creating a classroom environment in which all students have a chance to learn in their own way. In each case, the teachers collaborated with their student (or students) instead of formulating an intervention on their own. And because the students had helped to create the interventions, they followed through with the strategies.

The solution-focused approach presented in this section provides a new perspective from which to create an instructional climate that is based on respect for all students and the competence of all students, so that misbehaviors occur less and academic success occurs more. The first two chapters were written to inspire you, and the last two provide direction for Tier I interventions.

Chapter 1

Simple Addition

Doing Things Differently Adds Up to Change

What would a solution-focused approach to RTI look like on the elementary, middle school, and high school campus in your district? How would a teacher utilize a solution-focused approach to create a successful context in which challenging students performed masterfully? And how might each of those students respond to such a respectful and curious educator whose desire was to focus on their strengths rather than their deficits.

Let's take a look.

An Elementary Discovery

Alice Cedillo did not realize that her worries about getting everything done for the achievement tests had affected her students. As an experienced teacher, Alice had always completed things on time, but because she was now in graduate school studying for her school counseling certificate, things just kept piling up. She was frustrated and needed to get just one more thing done before going on to the next lesson.

So on that warm afternoon in Texas, her fourth-grade class did what any class with an unhappy teacher would do. They misbehaved. As she tried to settle them down, one of her students asked innocently, "Ms. Cedillo, are you okay?"

A bit taken aback by the question, Alice replied with her own question: "Why are you asking me this?"

The student responded, "Because you are yelling at us more than usual."

Alice Cedillo was known for her outstanding teaching, classroom management, and humorous attitude, which always made learning fun. So when she became a bit irritable, the students felt her pain and it rippled throughout the classroom. My, was she a powerful influence. She recognized that influence when the student spoke up, so instead of putting the blame back on the students and telling them they needed to behave, she did something different, innovative, and very solution-focused.

"Hmmm. You are probably right. What do you think I need from you right now that would help me?"

Hands flew into the air. Alice was amazed. The answers ranged from "You need us to be cooperative with you" and "You need us to be quiet and do our work" to "You need us to be nicer this afternoon."

Given these rather candid but sincere responses, Alice took the opportunity another step: "And what would that look like, just for this afternoon, in this classroom, when you begin being cooperative, quiet, and nicer?"

Again, hands flew up. By this time, Alice was at her whiteboard, writing down the students' suggestions, smiling to herself. She went over the suggestions again and repeated them back to the students, asking how they would each begin doing those things on a small scale just that afternoon. They told her what they could do. The rest of the afternoon went perfectly. Alice was amazed—so amazed that she used the same strategy weekly, sometimes daily, and added a rating question to the exercise: "On a scale of 1 to 10, with '10' meaning we are doing everything perfectly together that I want you to do, and '1' meaning we are not doing very well at all, where would you want to be by this afternoon?"

When the students took on the task of making their score go up, they also took on ownership. They became even more responsible than before, even when the typical reward and consequences were given out. They also seemed proud of themselves, which Alice was quick to acknowledge. Alice was impressed with the way the solution-focused approach to classroom management worked, so much that she began noticing that her mood was more stable and her class even more delightful. The students, in turn, responded the same way. After one year of using the approach on an almost daily basis, Alice decided to take the solution-focused approach another step.

In the fall of the next year, Alice wanted to create the same environment with her new crop of students. Normally, she required that students always ask to borrow scissors, pencils, erasers, glue, or any other item from her desk—a sort of boot camp training to make sure that she had things under control. Given her good experience in the spring of last year, she decided to try something else. She designated an area of the classroom for her students, saying, "This is your supply table. On it are all of the supplies you will need this year. I want you to feel free to get what you need when you need it. The thing is, you are responsible for keeping it neat and orderly. You won't have to ask to use these things. This is your privilege. You keep that privilege as you take care of things. I trust you."

The students took better care of *their* desks than any students in previous years had done to take care of the things they borrowed. She began to wonder more about the solution-focused approach and how different it was from what she had learned about behavioral approaches to classroom management and discipline. Could it be that this new generation of students could become responsible without needing an authoritarian environment? And could they become more respectful and compliant as a result?

Intermediate Revelation

In an intermediate school twenty miles away, Patti Gatlin, a school counselor, had concerns about her school client, Brian, who was returning from alternative school the next day. Brian had developed some behavioral issues over the past semester that had caused him grief and cost him lots of referrals to the office and the alternative school. While Patti had tried to gather Brian's team for meetings about how to support Brian, the team seemed to be at a loss on how to help him. Prior to this day, Patti had noticed that whenever Brian had returned from his previous stints at alternative school, it was with a good report; however, he usually rebounded back to his old habits after only a few days. This time, Patti was determined to do something different. She went to her principal and explained to him that there was a need for everyone, including Brian, to get a fresh start when Brian returned. Luckily, the principal was flexible and forward-thinking, and he said yes to Patti's request. That afternoon, Patti made Brian a new schedule. *When he comes in tomorrow,* she thought, *he is going to get a fresh start—and a new team.*

When Brian came in the next morning, he was anxious and concerned. He, too, wanted things to be different, but being an adolescent, he was rather stuck. When Ms. Gatlin told him he had a new team, he was skeptical but relieved. *Maybe this will work,* he thought. When Brian went to meet his team, he was impressed by their welcoming smiles and openness to helping him get on track. Ms. Gatlin told the team that Brian did well in alternative school both behaviorally and academically. He had the ability; he just needed a new context to show off that ability, and many of the teachers on his new team used a similar teaching style to that in the alternative school.

It has now been four months since the team change. Brian has had no further incidents with behavior. His teachers are able to teach Brian in the way that he needs to be taught in order to succeed. In a recent team meeting, Brian was assessed as doing well and it was noted that his grades are improving quickly. He was referred to as "pleasant."

Raising the Bar and Rating the Middle School

Ten miles away, on the same morning that Patti Gatlin held her first meeting with Brian's new team, the principal of a middle school couldn't wait to announce the results of the most recent state achievement test to the faculty. Excited and unable to contain her enthusiasm about the test results, she raved, "Some more great news—the passing rate for eighth-grade reading was 96 percent, which I told you about last week. What you didn't know was that the passing rate for the at-risk students was 92 percent. I learned at my meeting on Friday that our school had the smallest achievement gap for this subpopulation of any middle school in the district. That accomplishment was noted and discussed at the district meeting. Congratulations to Tonya Romine and her talented students!"

How did Tonya Romine, a teacher, single-handedly raise the achievement scores in a classroom full of at-risk students? I asked her, and she told me:

It began with one student who was at risk as well as enrolled in special education. I did an activity with my class, using the scaling question "On a scale of 1 to 10, with a '10' meaning you reached your goal and a '1' meaning you are far away, where are you?" I told students to put down on a paper the goal that they really wanted to accomplish. I said it could be something like passing TEKS (Texas Essential Knowledge and Skills) or passing eighth grade. I told them that it could be something small like turning in assignments or even using their planner daily.

Then I used myself as an example. I wanted to lose weight. If I tried to go straight from a "2" to a "10," skipping all the steps, going from eating terrible and never working out to strict healthy eating habits and working out every day, would that work? They thought that was really funny because they have seen me eat! I told them that the same concept works for them. They got it. Together, we wrote things they would have to do, calling them "small baby steps," and I asked them to keep their scales to refer to.

One of my students went from making C's in the beginning of the class to making all A's and B's. When I was going over his grades the next six weeks, his grades were amazing. I asked him about it. I asked, "How did you do that?" He said, "It was because of you, Mrs. Romine." It didn't occur to me that he was talking about the scale he had created. It had made a huge impact on him. We recently got our TEKS test scores back, and he passed! He had never passed the reading TEKS in the previous years. This was the first time!! He continues to be successful! One last thing: this was also his first year out of resource reading! I have now told him that I have full faith in him, that he can tackle any obstacles that come his way!! In one week, he has the math TEKS, and he says he is ready!

Out of the nineteen kids who took the TEKS reading test, only three did not meet expectations; six of the nineteen were special education students.

High School Miracle

In Oslo, Norway, over five thousand miles away from Alice, Patti, and Tonya, Vibeke, a high school teacher, had just learned about solution-focused ideas at a workshop. She dreaded going to class because there were two girls in her writing class that were bullying each other to the point that teaching had become a huge challenge. Vibeke had tried disciplining the students in her class, but the students rebuked everything she said to them. At the workshop she attended, she was introduced to the concept that there can be no resistance when a person cooperates with another person's needs. She also liked the idea of the miracle question. *I could certainly use one right now,* she thought. Approaching her classroom on Wednesday, Vibeke was ready to try something new.

The class entered the room, rowdy as usual. Instead of engaging in a power struggle to settle them down, Vibeke simply stood in front of her desk, quietly waiting until everyone sat down. The students were a bit surprised. Normally, there would be an assignment on the board for them do as they were settling in. Today, the board was blank. When the students were curiously quiet, Vibeke began:

> Students, I realize that I have not connected well with you this semester and that you are not getting what you need from me. There is a problem in our classroom with people being disrespectful, and I am in need of your help. Let's say that after you leave this classroom today and then go home, overnight, a miracle happens. When you return tomorrow to our classroom, things are much better. You can learn better, I can teach better, and everyone will feel more comfortable. What will be happening that will tell you that things are better for each of us?

Silence. When had a teacher ever asked her students for help? When had a teacher ever put control back into the hands of students in the form of rules or structure? The students sat silent for a long time. Vibeke was patient. Slowly, hands went up.

"People would be respectful to each other."

"School would be interesting. . . ."

"I could hear you teach us; it would be quiet."

"No more interrupting. . . . I would be listened to by the rest of the class when I had something to say."

"No name calling."

Vibeke was silently shocked at the students' answers. Some of the answers even came from two of the girls whom she had concerns about. Vibeke wrote the students' answers on the right end of the whiteboard. She then put up a scale of 1 to 10 and labeled "1" "challenged classroom" and "10" "great classroom." She asked the students to rate their class up until today. The answers averaged about 3. Vibeke thanked the students for their help. She said she wanted them to think about the exercise they had just done. Some of the students asked her if they could start some of their ideas that day. Vibeke told them that she wanted them to wait a day or two to think more about the exercise and that she would let them know when they would begin. On Thursday, the class was quiet and ready, but Vibeke told them that she still thought they needed time to think. On Friday, she told them that she thought they should try the ideas for that day only and see how things went. Things went so well that before the class was over, she asked them to rate themselves. They rated their class a "7."

The classroom ran smoothly for the rest of the semester. The issues between the two girls dissolved without Vibeke ever having to address them. Grades went up, and Vibeke, given more compliant students, became more creative with her teaching. The students actually policed themselves whenever a student tended to get off track. Vibeke's other classes joined in on the rating question, and a competition for the best classroom emerged on its own.

Turning Chaos into Compliments: A School Counselor Creates the Opportunity

Back in Texas, a second-grade teacher, new in her profession and full of optimism and patience, had started off the school year with a vision. The classroom was decorated with information about current events, student artwork, a couple of fish tanks, and a pet rabbit. The lesson plans were fun and informative. Yet at recess and eventually in the classroom, the angelic children in Ms. Juarez's class turned into bullies who threatened other students in their class and others outside their class.

By the time February came, Ms. Juarez's patience had turned to frustration and she asked her school counselor intern, Amanda Clark, to help her with getting her class back on track and regaining management of her class. Amanda was prepared to do something different as she walked into Ms. Juarez's class that morning. The students were a bit off task to begin with, and getting them back on some sort of orderly track seemed a tall order. Amanda put those observations aside, waited until the students became somewhat quiet, and spoke: "Hello, I am Ms. Clark, and I want to talk to you today because your teacher invited me to talk to you about some things that she was concerned about. Does anyone have an idea why I am here?"

The students' hands went up, each begging for a chance to reply, and Amanda answered each one, writing their answers on the whiteboard:

We're bad.

We pick on each other.

We aren't nice to each other.

We talk about each other.

Amanda quickly dispelled the idea that the children were bad, re-describing them to herself as "talkative, assertive, and generally off track." Her thinking kept her focused, open, and creative. Then, she asked them the miracle question: "Suppose tonight, while you slept, a miracle happened. When you came back to school tomorrow, what would be better?" Again, a flood of hands waved. Amanda wrote down different answers that the students gave to her:

We would be good.

We would be nice to each other.

We wouldn't start fights.

We wouldn't talk about each other.

We wouldn't pick on each other.

We would work together.

Amanda told the children that she really liked the last item that they gave her. She told them that they were going to play a game. She then divided the class into two groups. One group was to stand on one side of the classroom, and the other group would stand on the other side. They were to face each other. Then, Amanda gave each group a stack of construction paper. She asked each group to choose a leader. She told them that she wanted them to find a way across the room to the opposite wall by pretending that the construction paper was stepping stones. The leader was to begin laying "stones" (pieces of paper) one in front of the last, barely touching, until there were enough stepping stones to reach across the room. As the groups worked, they found that they could only get halfway across. They faced each other as both groups made it into the center of the room. There were no more sheets of paper to walk on. "We need more paper!" the students said.

Amanda told them that there was not more paper. Then she asked, "What are you going to do? How will you get to the other side?"

Silence. Then chatter. Then ideas:

"We can make both of our sides' paper touch, and then we can walk across."

"We can share the paper."

Amanda applauded their answers, and soon, the leaders of both groups spread their papers out enough so that everyone could cross over, both groups walking toward each other, then passing each other to the other side.

Amanda asked the students to go back and sit in their seats. She then asked them to tell her what a *team* was. The students began talking rapidly about what a team did. Amanda again wrote down their answers. She asked the rating question: "On a scale of 1 to 10, with '10' meaning you are a great team and '1' meaning you are not a team, where were you this morning before we did this game?"

Most of the children responded that they were about a "3" or "4." Amanda then asked the students what they could do to move up. The dialogue began to be about learning to be nicer to each other, being helpful to each other, and not picking on each other.

Amanda then asked, "Students, when you were doing the exercise a few minutes ago, who did you notice was already doing some of the things you just described?"

Hands flew up.

"Charlie did. He was nice. He's always nice."

"Juanita was nice; she shared the papers with me."

"Ken didn't punch me like he does sometimes when we crossed the room."

Amanda asked Charlie, Juanita, Ken, and others if they had realized they were being teammates. They smiled shyly and shook their heads.

There were many more compliments during this time than Ms. Juarez ever thought possible. As she stood there, watching the transformation, Amanda asked her to write the names of those identified as teammates on the whiteboard each day. She also asked her to rate the class on a daily basis. The students loved the idea of the scale and of getting their names written on the board in a good way. At the end, Amanda just asked the students to do whatever it took to get noticed by their peers so that more names would be written on the board under "Teammates."

Education Unleashed!

What happened to the traditional consequences, confrontations, and promises of an unfortunate future that any one of the teachers or school counselors in these scenarios had at their fingertips? They chose different options. They chose options that clearly took their system by storm and produced outstanding results. What were they thinking? They were thinking with a solution focus rather than a problem focus, and when it comes to Response-to-Intervention ideas, that focus on solutions opens up success for students who otherwise might never experience it.

New Focus, New Process, New Results

Solution-focused RTI is a process that involves less paperwork and more conversations that focus on solutions rather than problems. Are you sold already? Solution-focused RTI is

- A process that focuses on times when students are slightly more successful rather than times when they are unsuccessful, in prior years of school, current year at school, at home, or outside of school in extracurricular activities

- A process in which student referrals to special education are slowed down in an effort to identify competencies rather than problems, resulting in an appropriate decrease in referrals and increase in academic success

- A systemic process in which behavioral issues occur less and compliance and respect grow through a new type of relationship that develops between students, parents, and teachers

- A process that increases teacher competence and confidence as student resources are brought to the forefront, guiding teachers toward more effective interventions and thus ensuring more success

- A process that is less rigorous for staff and that invites more responsibility on the part of students and parents, contributing to buy-in by parents

- A unique opportunity for educators to see beyond problems toward solutions, increasing hope and an awareness of what works rather than what does not work

Because it takes a solution focus rather than a problem focus, solution-focused RTI may at first appear to be "just more positive." Caution! It is not simply more positive, optimistic, or simplistic. In fact, it is the opposite of simplistic, for it requires a paradigm shift in thinking for an educator. It will take the rest of this book to fully understand and put into practice the solution-focused way of thinking, acting, and responding. Understanding and implementing the process requires that you begin seeing success over failure, no matter how minute. It means counting minutes of success rather than thinking "He never pays attention." It means tearing up a note to a parent that describes a child's failure and writing a note that punctuates the child's assets, *even if those assets appear only occasionally.* Is this a softer approach? Not necessarily. But it is a different approach, one that challenges us to change our thinking from "She will never succeed in this class with her study habits" to "When does she study more efficiently, even slightly?"

Chapter Perspectives to Consider

In each situation discussed in this chapter, a traditional problem-focused approach might have had very different results. In the following perspectives, consider the differences in thinking that result from using a solution-focused approach rather than a problem-focused approach. Each change of thinking will lead to new strategies.

Teacher: What is my goal, and how can I enlist the help of my students to reach that goal? What can I do as their teacher to connect better with them?

Administrator: This teacher [or student] did not have a problem for the first three months of school. What was happening then that made a difference?

School counselor: How can I assist the teachers and students so that they see each other as competent and able to figure out what they would like to achieve?

Chapter 2

Famous People with Educational Challenges

Priceless Lessons for RTI

Solution-focused RTI asks educators to take a step outside a very comfortable box of familiar curriculum and behavioral plans in order to seek alternatives that will increase student success when those plans do not work. To do so, educators must view students through a new lens in order to discover interventions that have a better chance of working than problem-focused approaches. How much of an impact can putting on new lenses have on a student *and his teacher*? In this chapter, we will take a look at some very famous people who were perceived by their teachers as problem students destined to have less than successful lives yet, eventually, when given support and opportunities, excelled. In each case, teachers could have written off the student as learning disabled and denied all of us myriad inventions, entertainment, and productivity.

Perhaps there is a little Albert Einstein, Thomas Edison, or Terry Bradshaw in your classroom, hidden behind mischievous behavior or poor reading or math skills. What if you saw beyond the exterior difficulties of struggling students and saw their efforts, successes, and abilities—the exceptions to the idea that they have problems—just for a day?

Famous People Who Made It!

When you hear names such as Charles Schwab, a financial wizard; Ty Pennington, celebrity carpenter; Tommy Hilfiger, designer; Terry Bradshaw, athlete; Michael Phelps, Olympic star; Keira Knightley, actress; Dexter Scott King, son of Martin Luther King Jr.; Orlando Bloom, actor; Patrick Dempsey, actor; Whoopi Goldberg, actor; Albert Einstein, scientist; Thomas Edison, scientist; Jay Leno, comedian; Vince Vaughn, actor; Henry Winkler, actor; James Carville, political strategist;

Jim Carrey, actor; Nelson Rockefeller, financial expert; Harvey Cushing, M.D., neurosurgeon; Jewel, singer; John Irving, novelist; and Philip Schultz, poet, the last thing that comes to mind is "challenged." Yet these are just a few of the people who struggled in school and experienced various labels—such as *dyslexia* or *attention-deficit hyperactivity disorder* (ADHD)—that tended to keep them and their parents stuck. In this section, read about how some of them overcame their challenges and notice the ways that they adapted (in italics) so that they were not only able to get on track but stay on track.

Charles Schwab (Dyslexia)

In an interview with children asking about how he coped with dyslexia, Schwab mentioned that when he was growing up, there wasn't a label for his challenge. He said he hated to stand up in front of the class because he would always mess up. Memorizing a poem was impossible for him. He said he didn't read very fast so his book reports were always poor. But, he said, he was good in math and could count pretty well. He decided to emphasize his good side in math and not his bad side in reading. It sounds as if he chose the right side!

Ty Pennington (ADHD)

At one point Ty Pennington, star of "Extreme Makeover," was described as the worst child in the school. In an interview with *Ability Magazine,* Pennington explained that as a child he had an enormous amount of hyperactivity, which made learning difficult. He talks about being so out of control that he spent most of his time in detention or out in the hallway. He mentions too that at one point his mother, who was studying to be a child psychologist, was asked to come to Ty's school to test "the worst kid ever." To her surprise, it was Ty who walked in to be tested. Later, when his mother observed him in class, she understood. Thankfully, Ty turned his *active lifestyle into a creative one,* becoming the star carpenter on "Trading Spaces" and developing a wide range of home improvement products.

Tommy Hilfiger (Dyslexia)

Who would believe that the acclaimed fashion designer Tommy Hilfiger did not have a normal childhood or school experience? Hilfiger says, "I performed poorly at school, when I attended, that is, and was perceived as stupid because of my dyslexia. I still have trouble reading. *I have to concentrate very hard at going left to right, left to right, otherwise my eye just wanders to the bottom of the page*" (http://www.happydyslexic.com/node/20).

In reference to being the class clown, Hilfiger admits, "I didn't want anyone to know that I didn't get it" (http://www.happydyslexic.com/node/20).

Terry Bradshaw (ADHD)

Terry Bradshaw is a four-time Super Bowl champ and a commentator for Fox Sports, yet his life hasn't always been one of winning. "Perhaps his biggest challenge has been ADHD; he always found school and reading difficult. While Bradshaw did go to LSU largely because of his ability as a football player he was teased mercilessly about his low grades and his inability to read well. He admits that it was painful at the time, but instead of dwelling on it, Bradshaw simply put more of his efforts into his sport" (http://www.amazon.com/Its-Only-Game-Terry-Bradshaw/dp/0743509617). In his book, *Keep It Simple* (Bradshaw, 2003), he explains that *with treatment and support, ADHD doesn't have to interfere in his life.*

Whoopi Goldberg (Dyslexia)

When Whoopi Goldberg was a kid, they didn't call what kept her from learning dyslexia.

> They called it . . . you know, you were slow, or you were retarded, or whatever. And so, I learned from a guy who was running a program who I met one day and he had written out on a board a sentence. And I said to him, "You know, I can't read that." And he said, "Why not"? And I said, "Because it doesn't make any sense to me." So he said, *"Well, write down what you see under each. Whatever you see, write exactly what you see underneath."* And so, he brought me to letters by coordinating *what I saw to something called an A, or a B, or a C, or a D,* and that was pretty cool. (http://www.achievement.org/autodoc/printmember/gol0int-1)

Keira Knightley (Dyslexia)

Keira Knightley wanted to be an actress from the age of three. Yet her parents were wary of her entering the field at such a young age. Her problems in school gave her parents bargaining power!

> By the time she was 6, her mother struck a bargain with her. As the child had recently been diagnosed as dyslexic, she said that if Keira came to her every day of the summer holidays and spent an hour working on her reading and math, she would provide her with professional representation. This challenge was important. Up until this point Keira had been ridiculed by her schoolmates for her supposed stupidity. In fact, her dyslexia meant she couldn't read words and wrote numbers backwards. It got so bad that she'd get hold of book-tapes and memorize them so that no one would recognize her failings. (http://www.celebritytemple.com/keira_knightley/biography.php)

Jack Horner (Dyslexia)

Jack Horner was Stephen Spielberg's paleontological consultant for the movie *Jurassic Park*. He recalls struggling with math, reading, and foreign languages in school. Nonetheless, he loved science and was constantly searching for fossils. He looked at every science book he could find, yet never read them because he could not read. In high school, he won every science fair he participated in, creating innovative projects, but he still had problems memorizing answers for science tests.

> Jack reported, "I only remember one B in my life. The rest were a few Cs, mostly Ds, and lots and lots and lots of Fs. But I always believed in myself. This came from knowing that there were other things that I could do better than anyone else. . . . Throughout college, I learned a lot but I kept flunking out. I still couldn't memorize. It was also hard for me to keep up with lectures. In chemistry, I remember my teacher writing on the board and talking about something else at the same time. I couldn't follow either. And I could never keep up with all the reading."

> He got a job in paleontology at Princeton University fixing up all the dinosaur bones. It was there that he heard of dyslexia, to his relief. *Because I am dyslexic, I believe I offer a different approach to certain subjects. That comes with the way I think. I think differently, and that makes me ask questions differently.*" Jack advises people that if they are interested in doing something, they should spend time doing it. "But *do it your way; don't worry about other peoples' expectations.*" (Lauren, 1997)

Strategies as Unique as Students' Learning Differences: Discoveries That Work

In each situation described in the preceding section, a unique way of thinking, discovering, or coping on the part of the person involved led to solutions. While diagnoses such as dyslexia or ADHD give us reasons to get help for students, at times they are also a hindrance to us in thinking how we can help students, particularly those referred for RTI.

Recently, I spoke to a group of community college instructors who teach in Gateway to College, a unique and successful program that helps students who have dropped out of high school attend community college and gain their high school diploma and college credits at the same time. One of the instructors asked, "What do I do when students talk about their disorders such as ADHD, bipolar disorder, obsessive-compulsive disorder as reasons why they can't perform their schoolwork?"

This is an all-too-common question and situation. While diagnoses are intended to help students get services, they often become crippling to students *and their teachers* when staff members are pondering RTI strategies. When the diagnosis is glaring, it is difficult to see students' abilities. Struggling educators look beyond the students themselves and apply cookbook strategies. When those strategies fail because they weren't tailored to meet the real needs of a child, the child fails as well. Einstein's teachers thought he was a huge distraction to other students and demanded that he be removed from school and home schooled. Fortunately, his mother protested and demanded that he stay in school.

The solution-focused approach to RTI templates presented in the Tier II and Tier III parts of this book will not focus on the problem that has been brought to the teacher's or the RTI team's attention. Instead, the process digs in immediately to focus on the goal and then on the exceptions to the problem.

Whoopi Goldberg began to read slightly better with a different instructional directive. Jack Horner recognized that he had strengths that others did not and used his unique talents to become a paleontologist. Charles Schwab noticed that he had to read more slowly and carefully. To discover such unique approaches to helping a student learn and thus *to have the best chance of success, RTI teams must include the student and the student's parent (or parents)*. When a student and parent are on the team, the solution-focused approach emerges as a tool for looking beyond a problem-focused view toward solutions that will help the RTI program achieve its goal.

More Revelations

I recently asked a sister of a middle school student to accompany her brother to school for one week. Her thirteen-year-old brother was a client of mine who was struggling to get his work done, which was new for him, given that he had done quite well during his elementary school years.

The suggestion for his sister to accompany him was made after the brother said his sister was quite helpful to him in coaching him to do his work after school. *Why not have her try her coaching skills at school?* I thought. I actually did not think the brother would be the least bit excited about having his sibling accompany him to school, sit next to his desk, or walk with him through the hallways, but he was fine with it! After the week ended, I spoke to the sister about her experiences, along with her brother. While he had done quite well with her coaching, she was troubled by a few classrooms in which teachers tried unsuccessfully to gain some sort of control over the students. She said she wasn't surprised that her brother struggled in those classes. In a few classrooms, however, he was able to stay on track. Those classrooms, she said, had teachers who structured their classes, had high expectations, and, above all, developed relationships with their students. Her brother agreed. He said when he had structure and expectations he did not wander off with distracting thoughts. He also said having his sister along had meant that he had to stay focused. He said that in a few classes, his teachers kept him focused by checking on him randomly yet consistently. These observations gave me ideas and solutions to take to the student's school for a teacher conference. The teachers gained a sense of what the student needed and began implementing those strategies. Some teachers struggled in their attempts because their classrooms were not typically as structured as the student needed. The school counselor recognized the helpful strategies in the classes in which the student did well, and for the next school year, she placed the student in classes in which he could get the structure he needed.

Solution-Focused RTI and Diverse Populations

What would some of the famous people described at the beginning of this chapter say about how RTI could have helped them? I suspect they might suggest that if their teachers had thought outside the box more often, as Whoopi Goldberg's teacher did, they would have struggled less. Not all struggling is negative, however; sometimes struggles lead to exciting new discoveries such as the light bulb or the theory of relativity. Solution-focused RTI attempts to help educators sort out whether a student struggles because of a learning disability or whether other factors are involved. Given the current overrepresentation of minorities in special education, it seems more respectful to use a solution-focused approach so that identification of learning disabilities is not at the forefront of our interventions. In our schools, "African American students are identified with disabilities forty percent more often than the national average and are twice as likely to receive diagnoses for mental retardation and emotional disturbance. Native Americans are also numerically overrepresented in special education while Asian Americans are underrepresented. White and Hispanic students fall close to the national average. Across racial and ethnic groups males are diagnosed with disabilities at two times the rate of female students" (Swanson, 2008, p. 1).

In addition, a solution-focused lens can help educators to see past family issues such as incarcerated parents or students living with elderly grandparents who lack the parenting skills to assist with homework. Perhaps there are other people in a student's life who can escort him toward success. The student athlete who has difficulty in focusing on English vocabulary yet remembers his football plays may suggest that his coach has found a way to get his focus and help him remember. When given the chance to explore others in their lives who affect them best, students can be quite resourceful. I recall a student in fourth grade who was behind in reading skills and who loved to play with the kindergarten students. Because she needed to practice reading and the students needed to learn listening skills, pairing her up with a group of students two afternoons a week led to her desiring to read more fluently. The key is looking past the deficits that appear so easily and noticing times, places, and with whom students are more competent.

The possibilities for interventions in solution-focused RTI are as varied as the students themselves. While at first it's a bit scary to think that every student should be given individual opportunities to excel, remember that in most general education classrooms, only a small percentage of students require the additional help. The national average for special education students in a school district is 9 percent, based on the 6 million students in the United States who receive special education services. And when students are given additional support or opportunities, rarely do other students vie for the same opportunities, often because students are sensitive to the needs of their challenged friends. On more than one occasion, I have seen elementary or secondary school students who are appreciative of a teacher who goes above and beyond to accommodate a classmate who is troubled.

Chapter Perspectives to Consider

Teacher: Just because a student seems different doesn't mean he doesn't contribute to the world. I will watch certain students each day for exceptions to their difficulties, and when I see them, I will mention to the student through a note or comment that I saw them do something different.

Administrator: I recognize that when I take care of issues for teachers, sometimes I lessen their competency. Instead, for a week, when I get a referral for behavioral issues, I will ask the teacher how she has handled difficult students like the referred student before. I will also consider the times when I do *not* get referrals from that teacher and mention that competency when I can.

School counselor: My job is to encourage people to believe in themselves, and I can do so by refraining from giving advice and relying instead on statements such as "I can only imagine how hard it is to teach Jimmy when he misbehaves. Yet I have seen you deal with other students who are even more challenging, such as Evan, quite successfully. What did you do with him that seemed to work?"

Chapter 3

Who Says the Square Peg Must Fit?

David Epston, co-author of *Narrative Means to Therapeutic Ends* (White & Epston, 1990) once said in a workshop, "People get stuck when they try to fit a square peg into a round hole." In education, when the peg doesn't fit, we think, *See, this student can't or won't* instead of thinking, *Perhaps it is our system of holes that needs to change, so that pegs of different shapes can fit.*

This section of the book will review the solution-focused approach, a novel addition to education, which seeks to answer the question "When and where does school work for this student?"

Prior to this approach, asking such a question would be last on a list of other questions that would often begin with "Why can't Johnny read?" Today, seeking to know why frequently brings more referrals than solutions. This book aims to slow down referrals by looking into the worldview of students and their parents and seeking times when school works, even slightly, so that the system used will be one that works for students and parents.

Each of the educators described at the beginning of this book took it upon themselves to do things differently in order to create an environment in which they could teach all students. They designed classroom management and learning strategies with their students. They worked hard to get to know their students intimately. Most of them told me that it was truly different from what they had learned in their education classes because it involved taking a step back and involving students in a process that the teachers had thought belonged only to them. The result? Respect, ownership, and motivation among students increased, and teachers could get down to teaching *all* students.

How can a teacher, administrator, or school counselor begin to provide an environment that is conducive to learning for all students when there is so much to prepare and provide academically? The answer requires considering many points of view within a school. The next sections will provide examples of how the solution-focused approach enriches the systemic, classroom, and community perspectives.

Systemic Perspective: The Hierarchical Leader of the School Leads the Pack

The principal of a school who embraces the solution-focused RTI approach must encourage teachers to create a classroom management culture that prioritizes relationship building as the number one method of motivating students. This approach is different because it supersedes developing classroom rules, setting academic expectations, using behavior charts, and even preparing for achievement tests. Yes, there are benchmarks. Yet as Tonya Romine found, by helping students to change their thinking about themselves and learn how to set small goals, we can help them improve their achievement scores. Yes, there are lesson plans to complete and turn in routinely. But unless teachers take the time to get to know *all their students* and develop working, respectful relationships with them, things will stay the same. Students still desire to please their teacher, even though many of them rarely show that desire. And little progress is made in a classroom where the teacher is not respected. Granted, many students have few clues on what respect looks like because of a difficult home life or poor treatment in previous school years. We have to teach them through modeling and communication that spells out "You matter first, schoolwork matters second." While this approach is controversial, to say the least, what each of the educators described at the beginning of this book realized, quite by accident, was that their students would try their hardest when they knew that the person behind the desk supported them as a person and as a student.

Leading teachers is a difficult task. It is one thing to ask teachers to get to know their students, and it is another to know how they can do so. I recall consulting with a group of teachers in an intermediate school in which discipline was becoming a concern. Every afternoon, the detention halls were filled with unruly students. Staff morale was poor because school was all about controlling the kids. Parents rarely came to school except for parent conferences about expulsions. One afternoon, in a workshop with the principal present, I began talking about solution-focused conversations, which make students responsible for coming up with a goal, then strategizing on steps to take in order to improve their behavior. I mentioned that by developing a solution-focused conversation with a student, the teacher did not have to be the expert. The student becomes the expert on her own behavior and academic work.

I noticed several teachers looking at me with a puzzled expression, and finally, one spoke for her colleagues: "If we talk to students like this, we will be victimizing ourselves. We will be giving up our role."

Startled, I looked at her principal, who was also startled by the comment, and asked her if it was all right for her teachers to have such conversations with their students.

She stood up slowly and said, "I give you permission right *now*, to reach out to your students in this way and find out what they think they need and what we need to do for them. What we have been doing is not working."

This systemic shift was necessary to begin altering the climate of the school.

If you are an administrator or school counselor, strongly consider speaking to the staff at your school about this approach, making an effort to change the environment of your school to a more collaborative one. Glasser (1998) wrote, "The only way education is going to change is if the classroom teacher makes it happen" (p. 7). Perhaps teachers in your school need some permission to try out new approaches such as the solution-focused approach. Most teachers are struggling to improve their students' behavior and academic performance and are quite open to new ways of working with them. Typically, teacher education programs lack curriculum on problem solving, leaving novice teachers lost when students walk into their classroom with an array of family problems. To assist teachers in providing new ways to approach and deal with such problems practically guarantees a more collaborative, peaceful classroom. If you are an administrator, that means fewer referrals for you, and if you are a school counselor, it means more time to work on creative methods of classroom guidance and delivery of individual services.

Classroom Perspective: Engaging Students in the Solution

In the classroom, teachers must seek to engage students in a culture that cultivates their empowerment. This approach goes hand in hand with the systemic perspective, for a teacher who engages his students through creative lesson plans and a genuine personal interest in them gains respect. Respect is not gained when teachers overpower, bully, or criticize their students openly and candidly in front of other students.

I recently worked with a first-grade boy, Bradley, whose mother was very concerned about his behavior. Bright and articulate, he told me, "You don't get good notes at school, Linda, only bad ones. . . . Everybody gets bad notes." Listening only for *exceptions* to the notion that Bradley had behavior problems, rather than problems, I noticed that Bradley had had few problems in preschool or kindergarten. However, this year, his first-grade teacher reported many behavior problems and some academic issues and subtly suggested that Bradley's mother take him to be tested for attention-deficit hyperactivity disorder.

Yet in my encounter with Bradley, I saw intelligence and a young boy who played peacefully during the session, not interrupting his mother once as she talked to me. I kept pursuing more information from his mother on what had worked in previous years. She reported that in Bradley's preschool and kindergarten classes, there had been fewer children and a lot of structure and that both of the teachers had taken great interest in Bradley, who often stayed in to help his teacher when the other children went out for recess. Bradley's mother went on to say that his current teacher only said anything to him when he was doing something wrong. That's when Bradley stood up in my office and told me about the bad notes. The mother said she wished that the teacher would do more of what had worked in the previous classrooms. But in order for the teacher to do so, Bradley's mother realized that Bradley would have to do things differently. When I asked Bradley what he thought his teacher needed to see him doing differently in order for him to get a *good* note, he gave me quite a list of better behaviors:

He needed to pay attention.

He needed to finish his work before getting out of his seat.

He should be nice at the learning centers with other children.

He should help his teacher more.

He should not trip anyone in the lunchroom line.

Bradley came up with these ideas without any prompting from me. Even a six-year-old often knows what he needs to do to improve behavior and school-work. A six-year-old can help his teacher and his team come up with solutions for learning and behaving. Yet children of this age are often left out of the loop of team meetings and parent conferences and are simply told what they need to do differently. Nonetheless, their input is vital.

I asked Bradley to draw two pictures, one that depicted him doing things well, things that his teacher would appreciate, and the other one, not doing things well. One was a picture of a superhero who did fantastic things at school. The other was a monster who made mistakes at school. I asked him to choose the picture he wanted to take with him to school the next day. He chose the superhero. I asked him to show the picture to his teacher the next day. He readily agreed.

The next morning, Bradley's school counselor and I spoke on the phone (with Bradley's permission), and I shared the strategies that had worked for Bradley in preschool and kindergarten, such as a structured classroom, compliments, and good notes. The counselor met with Bradley and his teacher (at my suggestion) to discuss the ideas, and Bradley told them both what he was going to try and do, showing them his superhero picture. Follow-up meetings several weeks and then several months later found Bradley greatly improved and getting good notes. His teacher even commented to the school counselor that writing good notes was something she should be doing more often.

What about the other students? Sometimes when I suggest that teachers try something new and unique with a student, they retort, "If I give her a chance, the others will want a chance, too. It's not fair to give her a break."

I respond with another unpopular suggestion: "So if others need a break, let's give them one!" In Bradley's case, a kind note led to good behavior and other classmates were relieved of Bradley's antics. Instead of worrying about how doing something for one student might lead to doing things for others, it is more helpful to observe how changing a strategy or approach for one student will affect the others.

Remember Alice? She could have said to her disruptive students, "If you would behave today, I would be in a better mood." Instead, Alice took the time to ask her students what they thought she needed from them in order to create a good afternoon for everyone.

The same principles of trying something new, asking students for their solutions, and empowering them to change their own behavior also works well in secondary schools. When I was a high school counselor, I was often in trouble with my colleagues for changing a student's schedule when that student was struggling. My colleagues warned me that I would have a line miles long outside my office if I continued to change schedules. However, I didn't change a student's schedule unless our solution-focused conversation led me to believe that a change would work. Often, the student recognized that *he* needed to change, not the schedule. For those students, meeting with the teacher in question often took care of most of the issues.

Community Perspective: Getting Parents on Board as Experts

To be motivated to be involved in a school, parents must feel that their voice matters and that, ultimately, they are the expert on their child. Granted, getting every parent involved is a challenge. Many parents are focused on surviving, and unless an invitation is warmly extended to them, school may not be a priority. Still, parents often are not involved because they don't feel that their voice matters. They may be so used to getting phone calls only when their kid is in trouble or failing that they just let the phone ring so they don't have to hear the bad news.

While in graduate school, Carolina Benitez taught kindergarten at Santa Fe Elementary School in Cleburne, Texas. She shared with me how one night, two parents who were rarely involved with their child's school came to an open house at which science exhibits were featured. Surprised to see them, Carolina struck up a conversation with the parents in an effort to make them feel welcome. She learned that the parents were very interested in the science exhibits because they were fans of boa constrictors and had two at home as pets. Carolina, sensing their passion, asked the parents whether they would like to bring the creatures to school to show the children in their daughter's classroom. They accepted her offer! Since their initial involvement, the parents have been more involved in their daughter's academic life, and their daughter's grades have been improving drastically. Finding ways to see parents as competent has a ripple effect on their children. Consider the following ideas:

1. At the beginning of each school year, some teachers survey their students' parents in order to learn about their interests and profession and then personally invite the parents to school to showcase their talents and interests. This activity goes beyond career day. Integration of speakers into traditional curriculum spices up classrooms, makes parents feel that they are part of the school, and helps students to see school as important. And this activity can go beyond elementary school. During the middle school and high school years, parental involvement is crucial to children's good behavior and future development as adults. At first, secondary students may balk at such a survey, leaving it up to the teacher to e-mail it home to their parents or hand it out at registration. But typically, a secondary student whose parent comes to school to participate will be much more invested in school. This type of inclusion also helps to create buy-in from parents when teachers need their assistance later.

2. When a parent conference is needed because of an issue with a student, parents should not be called and told their child has a problem. Instead, the parent can be called in as an expert on their child. Such an invitation is more likely to be accepted if the parents see that the school wants to help by listening to their opinion. Later in this book, Level A, B, and C meetings will be described as opportunities for parents and students to participate in designing their own Response to Intervention. Including parents and students in RTI meetings increases the chances that a parent will identify times when school has worked better for the student and thus increases the chances of RTI success. It is one thing for teachers or educational experts to try to help a student by choosing research-based curriculum on their own and quite another for a parent to describe a specific learning modality or activity that helps their child. Once one or two strategies have been identified by a parent, teachers can then suggest a curriculum or activities that are similar to the ones identified by the parent, leading to a respectful collaboration among all the members of the RTI team.

3. Many wonderful teachers have found that writing competency-based notes home to parents about their children can produce remarkable results. Such an effort takes approximately a minute to do, but the effects can last a full semester. It is a proactive alternative to another detention warning, and its effects are as long lasting as the message is in print! What is it about a one-page note that can make such a

systemic difference? Read the following note, which was sent home with a student whose behavior was often troublesome to his fourth-grade teacher. The teacher began to watch for short amounts of time when the student had slightly better behavior and found it on the playground.

Dear Mr. Diaz,

I am writing you this note to congratulate you, as Juan's father, for rearing such a helpful son. Today, Juan saw another student sitting alone on the playground, and he went up to him and asked him to play kickball. It made the student's day. I am proud to have Juan as my student. I am going to watch for more times when Juan is helpful to his classmates. I am impressed!

Respectfully,
Kim Anderson

The chances are that when Juan takes his note home, he will get a good response back from his father, which will result in Juan seeing Ms. Anderson differently. Seeing her differently, Juan may make sure that good behavior occurs more often. By taking the time to look for some exceptions to his pattern of problematic behavior, Ms. Anderson helped Juan to see himself and his teacher differently.

Solution-Focused RTI Applications

As Davenport Community Schools went to work to implement the solution-focused approach, they adhered strongly to the suggestions made by Congress in the Individuals with Disabilities Education Act:

- Students are placed in the least-restrictive environment in which they can receive additional services from staff members.

- Parents are included in the process of their child's education and are seen as a resource.

- Staff members are trained to offer more services and strategies that support the needs of students who need additional learning situations.

- Students should learn with their peers unless their individual needs surpass what the classroom teacher can provide.

- Support staff from local area education agencies can assist the regular classroom teacher in helping students learn, thus allowing the student to stay in the general education classroom.

- Exceptions to students' problematic patterns, identified by staff, parents, and support staff, are key elements in the solution-focused intervention process in that they raise and stabilize general education teachers' expectations of their students. [Metcalf, 2008a]

Once educators recognized that the solution-focused initiative in Davenport was there to stay and that they had to get creative in order to implement many of the congressional suggestions, they not only saw more student achievement but also witnessed their own competencies develop. Committing to keeping students in the general education classroom as much as possible led to fewer special education referrals for academic or behavior concerns. Teachers were forced to find a way to accommodate students, and they did. As the Chinese proverb says, "Give a man a fish, and you have fed him for today. Teach a man to fish, and you have fed him for a lifetime." Teachers, students, and parents in Davenport learned to fish. So can you. Solution-focused RTI is not a cookie-cutter method or a specific structure. Instead, it is a way of thinking that capitalizes on students', parents', and teachers' strengths, abilities, creativity, and curiosity.

Chapter Perspectives to Consider

Teacher: Instead of thinking, *How can I help these individual students plus the other students?* I will think about how I multitask every day of my life as a teacher. How do I do it? How can I start slowly, multitasking to meet student needs, just for a week?

Administrator: Our teachers need support. They need to have less paperwork so that they can focus on the students. How can I reduce what they have to do administratively so that they can teach?

School counselor: How can I support the teachers and help them identify exceptions to problematic patterns? What if I sat in the classroom and observed what worked when a teacher taught a particular student? What if I wrote feedback on what she did that seemed effective for all students and for the struggling students?

Chapter 4

Guidelines for Solution-Focused RTI

Recently, an elementary school teacher became frustrated with a student in her classroom whom she described as "distractible and slow to write down his spelling words." She wondered whether he needed testing for learning disabilities. She had tried rewarding him for completing his work on occasion and giving him a consequence when he did not. It never worked when it came to his spelling words. She stated, "I have this student in my fourth-grade classroom who simply cannot get his spelling words written in less than thirty minutes, no matter what I do. He will even miss recess, as a result, but that does not matter to him. What is the most frustrating is that once the children have left the classroom for recess, he can write the spelling words down in five minutes! I am so frustrated."

This otherwise talented schoolteacher saw only one behavior: the student did not write spelling words with the rest of the children. Yet once he was alone, for whatever reason, he could do the activity competently. When I mentioned to her that I wondered how it was helpful when the other students left the room, she did not know. She had all kinds of theories—for example, that the student was distracted by other students or that he needed the students to go to recess in order to remind him that recess was occurring—but she had not asked the student. I told her that I was curious about how such a context was helpful to the student, and I asked her to ask her student.

Another teacher told me about a student who had been placed in alternative school for truancy. He rarely came to school there, either, which presented a growing concern for the staff. However, one day he did come to school, and before he left for the bus that afternoon, the principal had visited the class, talking about an interest of his: the first astronaut who had stepped on the moon. The principal mentioned to the student that he had forgotten the name of the astronaut. Noticing that the student was listening to his conversation with interest, the principal spontaneously asked the student to find out the name of the astronaut and tell him about it when he came back to school the next day. The student arrived the next morning with information on Neil Armstrong and told his teacher that he needed to report to the principal what he had found out. The teacher then came to my class, complaining about the student's attendance. As an aside, she mentioned that the student had come to school that day to report on Neil Armstrong. My eyebrows went up, and again, I mused, "I wonder how that assignment got him back to school the next day." Together, we made all kinds of guesses:

- Did the student need a male role model to take an interest in him?

- Did the student need a purpose for coming to school?

- Did he like the attention?

All of which were fine, but it wasn't really necessary to figure it out. Instead, it was important to simply notice an exception, a time when the student complied and was successful.

Put on a New Set of Lenses in Order to See Students Differently

To begin changing your lenses so that you can start identifying exceptions such as the ones in the cases just described to help you in the RTI process, do the "Advertising Success" exercise in the next section, either by yourself or with colleagues. This exercise is an excellent one to use in a faculty meeting.

Start looking for exceptions, and keep looking. As you begin learning to apply the solution-focused approach to your challenging students, it is important to begin applying the same ideas that were used in the exercise to *all* of the students in your classroom, as Tier I suggests. Try putting on a new lens when you are stuck in regard to how to help one or more of your students. Learn to stop, think, and watch for times, for example, when Sarah is not as talkative or is not bullying other students. What is the context in which these exceptions occur? Then, *ask* the student, with curiosity, "How were you able to do that?" Asking the question will spark the student's realization that she was momentarily successful and raise her awareness of how to behave in order to be successful. It will also be an opportunity to compliment the student, something that students at risk rarely experience. Then, ask yourself how you can begin to duplicate such environments or contexts within your classroom and thus help your student succeed. The next section presents some basic ways in which an educator can apply solution-focused ideas in order to keep classroom management on track.

Suggestions for Beginning the Solution-Focused Approach to RTI

1. Use all available resources to teach all students. This approach requires a shift in thinking about the student; consider the student's interests, abilities, talents, and successful activities at home, at school, and in extracurricular activities.

A third-grade student had trouble sitting long enough in his chair to complete his work. He preferred to be on the computer, perusing science programs that described dinosaurs and their habits of long ago. The teacher struggled to motivate Sean to stay in his seat and finish his work, often seeing him gravitate toward the computer. When she finally had a personal conference with Sean, she said to him, "I am trying to find a way to get you to finish your assignments. I am stuck. Can you help me to find a way to get you interested in doing your work?" After a few minutes of thought, Sean said he did not know what it would take. The teacher went on to describe that she noticed how much he enjoyed the computer program on dinosaurs. His face lit up, and he began to describe to her why he liked it so much. She asked him how often he would like to play the program each day. He told her that he would like to play it at least three times a day. She then asked him what he thought he could do to earn that privilege. Sean began having much better days at school.

Because the student is now involved in the process of discovering strategies for school success, a shift in thinking about the student is necessary. On the next page, an exercise is provided to assist educators in shifting thinking from deficits to strengths.

2. Use exceptions developed from solution-focused RTI conversations to choose research-based best practices in curriculum and instruction and do so in collaboration with students, parents, and colleagues and base them on exceptions. What makes the solution-focused process so unique and so successful is its focus on identifying *exceptions*. Exceptions are

- Times when problems occur less

- Times when a student does not allow a problem to interfere with her life

- Times when a student is able to overcome a problem and be successful

Exceptions exist everywhere at your school, and it may be tough to begin seeing them. In your classroom or office, there are students who constantly misbehave or stray off task, or at least it may seem that way. But what if, just for a day, you took one of those students aside and said this: "Shari, I know sometimes it is hard for you to stay in your seat. I know that you love to move! I also think that I may be missing some times when you do sit in your seat. Today, I am going to

Advertising Success: An Exercise

Think of a student whom you consider a potential referral to RTI. The student may have academic or behavioral concerns. List all of the concerns that you and others have:

_____

_____

_____

_____

_____

_____

_____

Now, pretend that you are going to advertise the student to other teachers on eBay. List *at least* ten competencies, abilities, strengths, and talents of the student that would make the student attractive to other teachers:

1. _____
2. _____
3. _____
4. _____
5. _____
6. _____
7. _____
8. _____
9. _____
10. _____

Based on the selling points that you listed, design how you (and your colleagues) might begin working with this student to enhance his or her learning or behavioral success:

_____

_____

_____

_____

_____

_____

_____

watch for those times, and when I spot them at least three times, I will send a note home to your aunt, telling her what a great day you had."

Perhaps, too, through a solution-focused RTI meeting, you learn that a student enjoys and participates diligently in his science class, particularly when he is paired with another student. This may give you suggestions for class management and lesson planning.

Another student may have a problem with writing in a legible manner, yet has impeccable computer skills. She may be a student who needs to do her class work on a computer.

Recently, a new movie, *The Blind Side,* showed how a student with some emotional and academic challenges stumped his teachers by not raising his hand in class or writing down any notes. When given a test, he turned it in blank. Many of his teachers thought he was mentally challenged and destined for failure. However, one teacher decided just to talk to him about her class and ask him some questions. She was astonished to hear him recall facts about her class, the assignments, and the textbook, precisely. She shared her discovery with his other teachers, who found the same result.

3. Use a team approach to develop and deliver strategies. Decisions made in solution-focused RTI are made by a team of educators, students, parents, and others who are involved in the student's school life based on identified exceptions and data collected through rating success on the ten-point scale. It is important, then, that the delivery of such strategies be carried out by all present in the RTI meeting. During the meeting, everyone involved, including the student, will brainstorm about how they will each implement the identified strategies. This "systemic" approach multiplies the possibility of success and involves everyone in the student's life.

In short, solution-focused RTI uses the three tiers in a unique manner. In the exhibit on page 35, see how additional solution-focused RTI processing can assist with the objectives of each tier at a glance. The interventions will involve both the individual teacher and team thinking outside the box, flipping from focusing on problems to focusing on solutions.

4. Gather a schoolwide team of teachers, administrators, and counselors each year to review RTI interventions and gather data on the success of the RTI program. This team may rotate all of its faculty members from year to year in order to increase an understanding of the process and not burden the same staff members again and again. Their role is to serve as reviewers, not conductors of RTI meetings.

5. Keep records of success for future teachers to review. I suggest that students who are involved in the RTI process be identified somehow in their cumulative folder, which might contain a temporary RTI file, perhaps bearing a sticker that reads "RTI in progress." This way, a teacher or administrator who has a question about a student would see the RTI sticker and know that the student is involved in an ongoing assessment. The file will also help teachers in the future to know what worked for the student, saving time and frustration year after year.

6. If a student is entitled to be tested and admitted to special education services because he qualifies under the guidelines for standard disability categories or noncategories, develop a solution-focused Individualized Education Plan (with parental input) and implement it. Conduct an annual review, and schedule a reevaluation after three years.

If the objectives for all three tiers have been addressed and the student has not improved as the team deems necessary, the student may be referred for special education testing. Students who are referred will benefit if the plans that were used at all levels of intervention are given to the special education instructor.

Core Ideas in the Practice of Solution-Focused RTI

In *Counseling Toward Solutions* (2008a), I wrote about using the solution-focused approach in team meetings, individual student meetings, groups, parent conferences, and crisis interventions. The strategies centered on discovering, *with* the student, a goal, then identifying *exceptions,* times when the goal occurred on a small scale. Together, the counselor, teacher, student, and other team members identified where, when, and how the exceptions occurred and then developed strategies based on the exceptions. This is more than "catching them doing things right." It requires educators to shift their mind-set away from a problem-focused, cognitive behavioral approach.

The basic principles that guide the solution-focused RTI process, adapted from the work of O'Hanlon and Weiner-Davis (1989), are outlined in this section.

1. Use a non-pathological approach to make problems solvable. Honestly, for most educators, the most challenging part of the solution-focused approach is breaking their loyalty to the problem-focused approach. It is, after all, everywhere, from day care centers to elementary school classrooms, where rules are pasted on the wall, to alternative school classrooms in secondary schools, where levels must be obtained for privileges. It is also all that we know. Yes, problem-focused strategies work . . . up to a point, but only for certain students and usually not those who need some long-term assistance. The strategies work for students who rarely get into trouble or occasionally forget to do their homework. They work when students have supportive family members who back up the teacher at school. But for the rest of our students, who are therefore most likely to be referred to RTI, they don't work. Those approaches have been tried, and when they failed, the

Solution-Focused RTI at a Glance

The basic ideas that follow explain how solution-focused RTI fulfills the expectations of districts that educators will gather data, develop strategies, and review outcomes.

Tier I

Objective: The teacher is to differentiate instruction, and provide instruction designed to meet the specific needs of all students.

Solution-focused RTI: On a scale of 1 to 10, with "10" being the highest, the teacher rates the effectiveness of lesson plans, delivery of instruction, activities, and incentives to succeed through self-reflection and student input on a weekly basis.

The teacher deletes activities that do not work and implements more of the activities that have been identified as ones that work.

Tier II

Objective: The teacher or team Implements instructional programs that are aimed at developing a student's skills through the use of groups or additional coaching.

Solution-focused RTI: The teacher or team finds out how colleagues approach challenged students with even slight success, and implements or integrates those strategies with research-based curriculum to raise the student's skill level. The teacher or team uses the 1–10 scale to rate the student's success in the classroom with the student on a weekly basis. The teacher or team inquires of the student and his or her parent how the student learns best, and searches for times and situations when the student is more successful, inside or outside the classroom.

Tier III

Objective: The teacher or team provides a higher level of instruction and evaluation to students who have not been responsive to Tier II interventions.

Solution-focused RTI: The teacher or team uses solution-focused conversation to continually seek exceptions, inviting the student and his or her parent to participate in team meetings. In addition, the teacher or team invites special education teachers to assist classroom teachers in applying research-based curriculum to exceptions. The teacher or team or diagnostician encourages exploration of health issues such as hearing, vision, or allergies.

failure label was placed on the student's forehead, pushing him further from success.

Using a problem-focused lens is easy; problems leap out at us and say "Here I am; her problem is . . . she can't read." Or "Here's the culprit: her parents are divorced, and no one encourages her to do homework." Or "Here he is in my office again; he hasn't got a chance. . . . His brother was the same way, and he is in jail." Yes, these problems are definitely culprits, attempting to keep students from succeeding and teachers from teaching. And focusing on the problem keeps everyone from seeing the student's exceptions.

When an educator goes looking for the following labels, students readily step up to the plate and show off their labels:

ADHD: attention-deficit hyperactivity disorder (the busy, distractible student)

ADD: attention-deficit disorder (the daydreamer)

ODD: oppositional defiant disorder (the inappropriately assertive student)

It is important, therefore, when using solution-focused RTI, to redescribe students so that our labels don't interfere with watching for better actions (White & Epston, 1990).

Consider how educators often *react* to problem-focused thinking:

Problem Focus	Reaction	Does It Work?
ADHD	Isolate	Rarely
Defiant	Lecture, refer	Rarely
Off task	Redirect	Rarely

Now, take the same behaviors from the "Problem Focus" column in the preceding table and re-describe them, compiling some thoughtful actions when using the new description.

Solution Focus	Action	Does It Work?
Energetic	Notice times when the student's energy does not interfere with learning. Notice times when the student is on task, and ask the student what was helpful during those times.	Yes, more likely as the teacher identifies situations, lesson plans, and teaching styles that are more effective in cooperating with the energy.

(continued)

Solution Focus	Action	Does It Work?
Assertive	Let the student know that you are interested in her ideas on cooperating. Watch for compliance, and compliment the student when it happens.	Yes, as it is a cooperative approach that will comply with a student's need to speak up in class.
Off task at times	Watch for times when the student is on task. Comment with curiosity, and listen for what works for the student.	Yes; it gives the teacher insight into exceptions that lead to on-task behavior. This discovery will aid the teacher in lesson planning and Tier 2 interventions.

New lenses plus new descriptions equal new options. When you are stuck, ask yourself, *How am I describing this student?* The answer may surprise you. Then, change it.

2. Always let the student (or parent) define the goal. If you have ever been frustrated because a student refused to do what you considered essential to their success, relax. You probably did your best. But it was *your* best, not the student's. If it's not the student's goal, they just won't try. I recall Juan, a student, once saying to me, "Look, I know I am supposed to like doing homework, but miss, I just don't."

I replied, "I don't really know *anyone* who loves doing homework either. But I'll bet there are other things you do that you don't necessarily like."

"Yeah," he said, "like chores and cleaning up after my dog."

"So, how do you manage to do that?"

"Well, I get an allowance for my chores, and I love my dog. Mom said I have to clean up after him to keep him."

Asking students "What will be better for you when things improve?" will give you some insight into what matters to them. In the following dialogue, the teacher used a solution-focused approach to find out what motivated a student who was failing his schoolwork. The same approach could be used with a student who is misbehaving.

Teacher: I know your parents are concerned about bringing up your math grade. I am, too. But that's what we want. How do you want things to be for you?

Student: I just want to be back on the soccer team. My parents say I can't play until I bring up my math grade.

Teacher: Wow. That's pretty important. What have you done before to get your math homework done or any other homework done?

Student: I do it when I remember to take it home. I just don't always remember.

Teacher: What kinds of things do you always remember to take home?

Student: My bicycle. [laughing] I like to race home.

Teacher: What else?

Student: My backpack. My jacket. My library book about dinosaurs. My dad and I read it sometimes when he gets home from work early.

Teacher: Hmmm. So you can remember some things. I wonder where you could put your math homework so that it begins to get home most of the time, since you always remember your backpack. Soccer sounds like a lot of fun.

This sort of dialogue will take the teacher from discussing her own goals to understanding the student's. While the teacher wishes that the student would be concerned about his math grade, she puts aside her goal and asks him about his goal. He wants to play soccer. Because the teacher is working with him to help him play soccer again, it is likely that the student will do things differently—because it is his goal.

3. Be aware that there is a ripple effect when one person changes that will affect the system.

James Wagley, a school counselor in Many, Louisiana, told me the story of an adolescent who couldn't care less about school. With black attire and long hair, he was often labeled a loser by his teachers and some local people. He did love the guitar, however, and he was quite good at playing it. James had tried working with the student to improve some school issues, to little avail. So when James learned that the student played the guitar, he spent their time together learning about the student's guitar and the songs he liked to play. They continued to meet for several times, just to get acquainted, without any mention of school. James also ran an after-school program, and he decided to ask the student if he would be willing to offer guitar lessons. The student was rather surprised at the request, but he accepted. He would attend the after-school program at a local elementary school and give lessons a few days a week. James told him that he could charge a small amount for his time. The student's parents agreed, and the student began teaching younger students. Within a few months, the student had cleaned up his appearance, to the point of cutting his hair. His grades began to improve as well. His teachers were stunned. The student was on his way.

What did it take for James to "look the other way," away from the problem, toward competencies? Perhaps the recognition that looking down the road of problems leads us to nothing but frustration and desperation. If you find yourself blaming someone else for a problem, such as a parent who is not responsible for her child or a student who simply won't work, ask yourself, *What is the description I have of this parent or student?* Then, CHANGE IT. The irresponsible parent becomes a parent who isn't focused on her child yet. The student who won't work becomes a student who has more important things to worry about. Then, keeping this new description in mind, extend your hand to each, saying, "What can I do to help you right now?" You may be shocked at the answer. The ripple effect will occur in each of these cases because you have taken the time to build a relationship. Don't be surprised if they tell you they don't know. Smile and say, "Okay, then think about it. I will ask you again in a few days. . . . I know you have a lot going on." Then, ask them.

4. Remember that it is not necessary to understand or promote insight to be helpful. Most of us have sat around at a meeting with parents, a diagnostician, a school counselor, teachers, and an administrator, trying to understand why Johnny can't read or why Shannon can't sit still and focus on her work. Divorce, custody battles, depression, sexual abuse, anxiety, frustration, shyness, and learning disabilities all become part of the question about why Johnny or Shannon is not succeeding. Time and funding are spent, assumptions are made, and research-based strategies are defined and then applied to Johnny and Shannon. Three months later, another meeting. Same issues, some improvement, but not much. "We need to refer." Parents are terrified, fearing the worst; teachers are reassured that it's not their fault that Johnny or Shannon can't succeed. Neither Johnny nor Shannon have set foot in a meeting yet, but their fate is decided.

There will never be enough time in schools, given the way they are structured, to take care of all of the services that students need. And I am convinced that taking the time for all the adults to figure out why Johnny or Shannon can't succeed is not helpful, anyway. What is helpful instead is learning when and where Johnny and Shannon are successful.

If given time, Johnny may disclose that things are loud at home because his older brother is always in trouble and his parents are always screaming at him, keeping Johnny from having anywhere to do his homework in peace. When given time at school, Johnny gets his work done in the library, where things are quiet. His teacher mentions in this meeting that Johnny does quite well with the younger students on the playground, always showing them how to play kickball. Together, the group brainstorms the idea that Johnny might sit in on a classroom two grades lower during reading instruction. Johnny is told that he can read to other students in that classroom as a bonus.

Shannon, it seems, has always been "busy" and has always found it difficult to stay seated. When asked by the teachers about times when Shannon sits for short amounts of time, her mother begins to chuckle and says, "Rarely." Upon further exploration of all of Shannon's classes, however, the teachers discover that Shannon sits in the band hall for forty-five minutes each day playing her flute. When asked how she does that, Shannon talks about the rules of the band instructor and the fact that she wants to be first chair, which she has achieved. The group decides to invite the band teacher into the meeting. Once there, the band teacher raves about Shannon's ability to pay attention. The group explores other areas in which Shannon concentrates and soon learns that she does best with lots of structure, clear expectations, and the knowledge that she will be able to get up and move at a certain time.

Everyone leaves a little more hopeful, without knowing why the problems happened in the first place—and this was achieved by identifying when the problems were not there.

5. See students, parents, and families as having complaints, not symptoms. Students, teachers, parents, staff, administration, secretaries—they get stuck. And when they get stuck, they begin wondering what they did wrong. Michael White, a narrative therapist, used to muse that life was like a pathway with a few boulders that occasionally throw us off path. Of course, we hate those boulders and are happy to get around them. Yet each time a new one is dropped in front of us, we sigh and wonder how we will get around this new one. "Turn around and look behind you, at all of the others you have already passed by," said White. "There are the answers."

Usually when we are stuck, it is because we do not have a goal or direction. So ask. Ask yourself, your student, the parent, the administrator, "What are we trying to accomplish?" Once you have the answer, do something different. For example, if a student is not passing his math class, and you have tried every intervention you can think of, ask what you are trying to accomplish. Then, if the answer is something like "to get the student motivated to like math and complete the work," try something different:

- Find out if there are classes in which the student *is* motivated and turns in work slightly more often. What's different in some of those classes? Ask the teachers what they do.

- After talking to the teachers, praise the student on his success in some of his other classes and ask what he thinks happens in those classes that helps him. Ask how you can implement those ideas in your classroom. Ask him how he manages to comply with the other teachers: "How do you do that?"

- Tell the student your dilemma: "I'm stuck. I see you as a bright student who merely needs to turn in homework to pass math, yet you forget. What can I do as your teacher, just for a day, to get you on the road to passing again?"

The idea is to see past symptoms or problems toward exceptions, the times when problems occur less.

6. Cooperate with the student's worldview, lessening the student's resistance. When Lance started drawing his video game characters in math class, his fellow students knew that he would not be working that day. A fourth grader who adored playing video games enough to memorize how the characters looked, he was a talented artist who often drew his way through the day, particularly in math class. His teachers had tried to get him to stop and do his math work. He would often comply, but then he would get to drawing again until class was over and his work was incomplete.

His teacher, Ms. Harrison, a young and creative type, was open to suggestions when she approached her school counselor for help. When the school counselor heard about Lance, she began wondering what the drawing did for Lance. She knew he was left alone a lot because both of his parents were realtors and worked late into the evening. She also wondered about finding a way to cooperate. She suggested to Ms. Harrison that she find a place where Lance could draw in math class as a reward for doing his schoolwork, one paper at a time.

At first, Ms. Harrison wondered whether this would be a reward. *No,* she thought, *but it will be a way to cooperate with who he is. A way to reach him and step into his world so that he wants to step into mine.*

Ms. Harrison had a hard time thinking of what she could do. That afternoon, while she was preparing for the next day, she noticed that Lance had drawn a monster on one of the math transparencies that she used for instruction. She had an idea.

The next day, she asked Lance if he would like to decorate her transparencies. The rest of the students loved the idea. Lance was taken aback by the request. It would mean that he would have to do the work that was shown on the transparency and turn it in, and then she would give the transparency to him and he could draw around the edges of the assignment on the transparency. She promised to show the students Lance's work the next day. Of course, she had offers from other students to draw, which, coupled with the requirement that the work must be done first, led to other students' finishing their work. Her room became a gallery.

7. If something works, don't change it; if it doesn't, do something different. Alice Cedillo could have confronted her students about their misbehavior in class that day that she was overwhelmed with the achievement tests, but that would have just been more of the same. Instead, she put the whole situation back on the students. She did something different.

Patti Gatlin could have returned Brian to the same team of teachers when he returned from alternative school, in the hope that he had learned his lesson. But she knew that would be doing more of the same. Instead, she did something different.

Tonya Romine could have lectured her students about the importance of an education and achieving goals in their lives and then told them that their grades had to be improved. Instead, she talked to them, used rating questions, asked them what their goals were, and discussed small goals and big goals and even her own goals. She did something different.

Vibeke could have sent two unruly girls to the office for discipline so that she could teach her class. If she had, however, the chances are that when the girls returned, they would have glared at her, had it in for her, and continued to disrupt her classroom. Instead, she did something different.

Ms. Juarez could have done a lesson on bullying, describing how bullying hurts others. The children might have filled out the worksheet, colored the pictures, and then left the room at recess to bully some more. Instead, she focused on what bullies often need to help their insecurities: leadership opportunities and compliments.

In each case, things improved, mostly because the students, given a different context, wanted to change. In RTI, too often, we rely on tried-and-true recipes for strategies that work on many students but not all of them. Doing something different means looking for opportunities when something different can occur. Recently, a kindergarten student, Dillon, was brought by his parents to counseling because he was in danger of being retained, mostly due to immature behavior. While in my office, Dillon was quite mature, polite, and cooperative with both me and his parents. I began wondering aloud what it was that I needed to be concerned about. His mother told me that in his kindergarten class, his teacher was terrific, giving the students free rein in their exploration of centers and activities. School was to be fun, touted his teacher, yet she was concerned that Dillon could not stay seated long enough to do his schoolwork. He often teased the other students and got distracted enough that he wandered over to the centers to play. Dillon's father mentioned that when he had visited the classroom for the first time, he had felt overwhelmed. "It is like a forest, full of toys and pictures and activities. I couldn't stop looking at everything. I began realizing that maybe Dillon just had too much stimulation." With this in mind, the parents began to talk about how different Dillon was at his church day care on Sunday, where things were not nearly as stimulating. Together, we talked about academics, and both parents said that academically, Dillon was doing average. They emerged with a plan to enroll him in tutoring during the summer and to place him in first grade, requesting a teacher with a more laid-back personality and a structured classroom with fewer distractions. The school counselor was quite helpful in making that happen.

8. Go slowly, focusing on strengths and abilities in the situations in which the student is successful. Are you different at home than you are at school? I hope so. So are your students and their parents. For many, home is a haven where an array of traits come out that don't surface in other places. Recall the adolescent who played the guitar that led to school success? What about the third-grade boy who walks his kindergarten brother to class then goes on to his class, every day, without fail? The same student may forget to put his homework in his backpack to complete that night. What about talking about his amazing memory to walk his little brother to class? How does he remember? Is it a habit? Who knows what he will say.

I recall working with a fourth-grade student, Les, who had developed tics. His face would contort sometimes, and another student in class would make fun of him. My client was terrified of going to school. What if the medication didn't work? he worried. His parents assured him that they were doing all they could and that he had to go to school.

So I went to school with him too. I asked to speak to the other student, Mark, who often made remarks to my client. I took them both to an empty office, and our conversation went like this:

School counselor:	Hi. I just wanted to talk to both of you for a few minutes. Do either of you have an idea why I asked you both to talk to me?
Les:	Yeah, he makes fun of me.
School counselor:	Really? What's that like for you?
Les:	Makes me not want to come to school.
School counselor:	Mark, did you know that Les felt that way?
Mark:	Nope. But his face does weird things sometimes. It's funny.
School counselor:	Yes, it does. You know, you seem like a nice kid. Do you laugh at other people, too?
Mark:	Yeah, sometimes.
School counselor:	Like everybody?
Mark:	No, I don't laugh at the special education students; they can't help what's wrong with them. My brother is in one of those classes, and my mom says we should not laugh at them.
School counselor:	Wow. Did you know that Les can't help the way his face twitches sometimes?
Mark:	I thought he was doing it on purpose.
School counselor:	Les, do you?
Les:	No. I even take a pill to stop it, but it doesn't always work.
School counselor:	What's that like when it doesn't work?
Les:	I get embarrassed and don't want to play with anyone.
School counselor:	What do you wish happened then?
Les:	That people wouldn't laugh.

Mark was surprised at Les's situation. He never laughed at Les again; instead, when others laughed, Mark corrected them. Looking for Mark's strengths in other areas gave me a way to connect his competencies with the task at hand.

9. Notice how and why behaviors happen, and always ask curiously, "How did you do that?" Asking "How did you do that?" reinforces and promotes change. The hardest part is noticing when Johnny completes his work, when Shannon sits still for ten minutes, when Adam does something kind for a friend whom he normally picks on, or when Jill doesn't throw a tantrum after she is told she must not take Kim's markers without asking.

And take it a step further with yourself. Notice when students are on task in the classroom. Are you walking around or behind your desk? Are you using the smart board or showing a picture book? Are you talking about yourself and an experience you had during a thunderstorm or just showing pictures of clouds? Are you wearing a mask while reading a storybook or reading in a monotone voice? These questions matter because they show you what works and, thus, what to keep doing. In fact, why not ask your students each Friday what you did during the week that they enjoyed? Afterward, integrate their feedback into your lesson plans as you plan the week.

Take the time to ask your colleagues what they do with Kevin or Kala that seems to work. Be open to trying new ideas that work for others; your students will benefit.

And don't forget to smile and appear surprised when your students tell you what they did that worked that day! Give them all the credit. Scratch your head and be amused at their discovery. There is no better positive reinforcement than that!

10. Realize that change is constant, and help students and parents to notice changes, too. As I have been discussing throughout this chapter, seeing changes takes a new lens. It means walking into your classroom first thing in the morning and seeing a note on your desk that reads, "Watch for exceptions today."

It is easy to see what does not work. But observing what does work does two things:

1. It gives you hope, and when you are hopeful, you actually encourage good things to happen through your attitude. That rubs off on kids.

2. It gives you strategies to use again and again. By watching for times when Shannon sits still, James stays on task, Kimmie doesn't hit Sheri, and Juan remembers his homework, you set the stage for more of the same.

The solution-focused approach, when applied to RTI, is a real leap out of the box of education and into the world of our students, asking and consulting them about the ways that they learn best. While the youngest of learners in kindergarten or first grade may not be prolific in explaining what they need, the chances are that their parents will have information about what has worked for their child in preschool or at home. Early elementary and middle school students are quite good at verbalizing what works with them and what does not work, as are their teachers and parents, although some have difficulty focusing on what does work versus what does not work. High school students often look back to their middle school or elementary school days when they are asked to provide examples of teachers who made a difference. They know what works, and they remember the teachers who did what worked.

While it sounds different to construct a process in which students begin to inform us how to help them in RTI, the time is right for such innovation. If educators use the solution-focused tenets explained in this chapter and look through a new lens to see students differently, their students' results will also be different in the days to come, and their school will come closer to being an environment in which all students can learn.

Chapter Perspectives to Consider

Teacher: Check for success during class. Ask your students what is working in regard to certain lessons and activities. Check on your own success in the classroom, recognizing which lessons worked best.

Administrator: Change team interactions into solution-focused conversations, working with parents and students toward solutions rather than examining problems. Always include the student in any team meeting! Be curious about what works, not about what is not working. The ripple effect will reward you.

School counselor: Review student data differently. Look for strengths instead of weaknesses. Build opportunities to witness success with all of your students as often as possible so that when concerns arise, you can inquire about past successes.

Tier II

Targeted Instructional Interventions

Students who do not succeed with the activities prescribed for all students in Tier I may be referred for Tier II services, which consist of more strategic interventions that often involve group tutoring or coaching. Typically, "Tier II interventions serve 5–10% of the students in groups of five students or fewer" (Education Service Center, Region 20, 2007). Tier II interventions supplement instruction in the core curriculum provided in Tier I. Specific interventions are provided by trained staff, and progress is monitored on a consistent basis. As students enter Tier II interventions, their progress is constantly monitored by their teacher and a team of professionals, who must determine whether students are responding to the individual interventions. Data collected through close monitoring is used to determine whether the student continues in Tier II or is referred to Tier III, which is a more intensive and evaluative process.

Chapter 5

Flipping the Coin in Education

The solution-focused approach to RTI is a radically new approach; instead of placing the educator in the role of expert with research-based interventions, it invites students and parents to assist educators in designing the solutions. Discussing problems is typical in education, but rarely does that primary discussion offer solutions that work for both students and staff. Instead, a checklist is often used to determine the problem and consider a possible diagnosis such as ADHD, depression, or anxiety, and then a recipe of interventions that might help is applied. Sometimes those interventions help, but more often they do not, particularly when a lack of motivation is a culprit. When that happens, the student, parent, and teacher are often left to assume that if a research-based intervention failed, it must be the student who is flawed.

By flipping the coin, we can take another look at the same kind of meeting. Instead of seeking what is wrong with a student, a solution-focused approach seeks times when things work better for the student. Becoming solution-focused means being curious about strengths, assets, and competencies, especially when such traits lie dormant within a student.

It's Your Call

We have a choice as educators. We can call "tails" and target the problem or "heads" and target the solution. In any gambling game, one would rarely try the same strategy over and over and over if it did not lead to any success. Elliott Connie, a solution-focused therapist, once told me of his experiences playing baseball in high school and college. He would have good games and not-so-good games. When he went to practice as a young player after a not-so-good game, he would always wonder *What did I do wrong?* Yet his coach never spoke of his or any other player's mistakes. Instead, he showed them videotapes of the good games. When Elliott asked his coach why he did not refer to the mistakes they made, the coach asked, "How would it help you to see what you did not do well? Watch the tapes of when you were successful and repeat the good plays."

In education, flipping the coin and doing things differently by focusing on what's working allows the student to lead us to new, innovative solutions, and *then* we can suggest ideas about which research-based interventions might apply. Remember Bradley, the six-year-old who noticed that only bad notes were being handed out? He knew that simply knowing that he could get a good note would inspire him to do better. The teacher had placed Bradley on a behavior plan, and when it did not work, she encouraged his mother to get him tested to see whether attention-deficit hyperactivity disorder was causing his distractibility.

Stepping back and seeing students differently—not as problem-laden kids but as kids who need help in identifying what works for them—is solution-focused RTI. When interventions are developed by students and their parents, their buy-in is priceless to all involved. The hardest part for educators is to learn how to step back and sit on our hands while observing times when students are slightly more successful. What will that look like? It will look like a conversation.

Conversation Template for Solution-Focused RTI

So far, you have been provided with some theory and many stories of success. By now, you are probably beginning to recognize a process that occurs in each of the stories. The following form, "How to Focus Your Conversation on Solutions," is a conversational template that will appear in various formats throughout this book. Glance at the form for an overview of the process that solution-focused conversations follow. The process outlined on the form can be useful in conducting individual conversations with students, parents, or colleagues and serves as a basis for Tier II and Tier III interventions, which will be explained further in the rest of the book.

How the Process Works

Let's review the basic steps in the *Steps That Create a Solution-Focused Direction* in the "How to Focus Your Conversation on Solutions" guide and learn how they work.

How to Focus Your Conversation on Solutions

Step 1: Talk About the Concern

"What can we talk about *right now* that would help you [or your child] to be more successful? I care about what you think and what you need from me."

_____

_____

_____

Step 2: Set a Goal Together

"Tell me what it would look like on a small scale when things get better in the near future."

_____

_____

_____

_____

"What difference will that make?"

_____

_____

_____

Step 3: Identify the Exceptions Together

"Take me back to a time when a little of that happened. What was different then? What did you do differently? What did other people do?"

_____

_____

_____

_____

(continued)

Step 4: Ask the Scaling Question

"On a scale of 1 to 10, with '1' meaning that things are not working and '10' meaning that things are perfect, where are things now in relation to your goal?"

_____

_____

_____

_____

_____

Step 5: Set a Task for a Short Time Period

"On that same scale, where would you like to be in [one day, one week]?"

_____

_____

_____

_____

_____

"What can you do to begin to make that happen?" (Go over the exception list as a reminder, if necessary.)

_____

_____

_____

_____

_____

Source: Adapted from Metcalf, 2008a.

Solution-Focused RTI

Step 1: Talk About the Concern

"What can we talk about *right now* that would help you [or your child] to be more successful? I care about what you think and what you need from me."

Whether it is a parent conference, a student conference, a team meeting, a staff meeting, or any other type of meeting, people have agendas that they want to talk about. Too often, however, educators lead conferences by bringing up issues that are not helpful. Such conversations rarely lead to solutions. Instead, they belabor the problem's influence on the student and create a climate of despair. If instead, the preceding question is asked, each person has a chance to pick out the most important item to work on. When a student's (or parent's) opinion is honored by giving her a chance to talk about her most important issue, the student (or parent) is more likely to be motivated to work on that issue later, because it is her own goal, not the teacher's goal. In solution-focused RTI, it is essential that students and parents be heard and that their goals be verbalized and received as important. When our goals are put on students without their input, the result is not favorable. But incorporating their input in the intervention creates buy-in on the part of the student (after all, it was *her* idea!), and parents feel that the school is respecting both of them by asking for their input.

Another selling point of asking the preceding question is that it serves as a freeway to the goal of both parent and student, shortening the conversation and speeding up the process of designing interventions. If you have ever conducted a parent conference, stating your concerns and talking about the remedies and then, thinking you were finished, heard from the parent, "One other thing that I really wanted to talk about is . . . ," resulting in an additional thirty minutes of conversation, you will appreciate the effectiveness of the question.

Step 2: Set a Goal Together

"Tell me what it will look like on a small scale when things get better in the near future."

There is nothing like a clear picture of where we are going to facilitate getting there. As an educator, you may have ideas about what it will look like when Julio begins doing his work more successfully. He will complete all of his homework, sit up and pay attention in class, ask for help, behave appropriately, and stay focused. But that is your goal. A parent may give this reply: "I won't get phone calls from the school as often. He will be passing his classes, and his father will be pleased with his good grades."

These two goals don't exactly match, do they? And unless Julio's mother's goal is honored, she will leave the school feeling less competent as a parent. To assist her in feeling more collaborative, consider responding this way: "Great! What do you imagine Julio doing in class and at home so that you don't get as many phone calls and he is passing his classes?"

She may reply, "I suppose he will be paying attention, doing his homework at night (with me working with him), asking you for help during class, and, definitely, behaving better."

To which you can reply, "That's a great suggestion. What difference will that make?"

She may say, "I think he will know that we are behind the school and that both his father and I expect him to behave and do his schoolwork."

The solution-focused approach to RTI works when parents and students work with us on their goals, which are often similar to our goals, in developing solutions.

Step 3: Identify Exceptions Together

"Take me back to a time when a little of that happened. What was different then? What did you do differently? What did other people do?"

Exceptions are times when school has worked better, whether it was last year in preschool (remember Bradley?) or in third grade, when the teacher was more structured and specific. Searching for exceptions takes time. When you ask these questions, always be ready with a question of "What else?" and repeatedly ask that question *at least five times*. By asking these questions, you force the student, parent, and teachers to seek times when school has worked. These exceptions will become the backbone of the RTI strategies that you will develop and even, if necessary, use for developing an Individualized Education Plan (IEP) later in this book.

As a facilitator of the RTI process, at times, you may find colleagues, parents, or students slipping back into discussion of what the student is doing wrong, such as "he runs around the room." When that kind of remark occurs, learn to ask, "What was different at times when he wasn't running around the room?" This strategy keeps you from interpreting and encourages more thoughtful discoveries of what was different in contexts when running didn't have a chance to happen.

Identifying exceptions is a key component of the solution-focused RTI conversation. By taking time to get specific instances of when school works better, the tasks that develop from the exceptions will be more effective.

Step 4: Ask the Scaling Question

"On a scale of 1 to 10, with '1' meaning that things are not working and '10' meaning that things are working well, where are things now in relation to your goal?"

This question helps to gauge where everyone is in relation to the problem. On more than one occasion, while asking the rating question, I have been amazed at the score indicated by students and parents. I have thought to myself, *I'll bet they see the student at a "2."*

Then, I hear a score of "5."

When I ask, "Why do you see your son at a '5'?" the parent answers, "Well, he has done better this semester than the last. He has the ability; he just doesn't try."

At that point, I can respond, "What can he do to begin moving to a '6'?"

It is also helpful to ask the parent or student how the teachers involved can assist the student in moving to a "6" as well.

Step 5: Set a Task for a Short Time Period

"On that same scale, where would you like to be in [one day, one week]? What can you do to begin to make that happen?"

These questions lead the parent and student to begin brainstorming about what needs to happen in order to raise the student's score. Their identification of what needs to change or occur is typically much more realistic than any idea I may have and, again, it is their idea. People try their own ideas. And they get the reward when their ideas work. Notice, too, the short duration of time suggested for trying out the new task. Why not go an entire semester or an entire school year? Because asking a student or parent or teacher to do that is too overwhelming. Short-term goals have a higher chance of being successful. Solution-focused RTI meetings are held every three weeks, and the rating question is the data-gathering instrument that is used several times per week, keeping paperwork brief and on task.

Now, let's apply the solution-focused process to a meeting held often at all levels of education: a meeting to develop a 504 plan (which outlines accommodations for students with disabilities under the Rehabilitation Act of 1973).

Flipping the Coin: A 504 Meeting

When I was a high school counselor, I was assigned to be the 504 committee chairman at my school. I remember perusing the 504 checklist that I was supposed to take into 504 meetings with students, parents, and administrators, eager to see which of the items on the list would apply to what students said they needed. However, I often found that the items on the checklist were not mentioned by the student. So I tossed the checklist and developed a different form that fit the solution-focused approach. While writing this book, I consulted with several RTI directors from local school districts who said that the education system needed to "flip a coin," so that the student had at least a 50–50 chance of being successful. Most of the time 504 meetings were held to talk about deficits and then apply a list of modifications. The form that follows, "504 Conversation for Success," is shown on the next page.

I carried out the role of 504 chairman that year, and not once did I have a student say that he wanted less work or a new school. Instead, answers to the miracle question led to strategies that appeared on forms like the "504 Meeting Summary for Teachers." Reproducible copies of both forms are provided in Appendix A.

The student-generated interventions and strategies that I received often required minimal teacher involvement. The responsibility was usually on the student either to verbalize what she needed from the teacher or to elaborate on how she would begin doing things differently when the teacher accommodated her request. Because the students had identified their own strategy, they seemed to see their contributions in a contractual way. Occasionally, there would be a goal such as "I would have a different teacher—one who is easier." While a transfer was not always possible, I still honored the student's request with the question "How would that make a difference?"

Usually, the student replied that he didn't feel the current teacher liked him and therefore did little to help him. I would explore further what the current teacher would be doing during the miracle day, and the student would describe new actions that the teacher would take. This description would become the statement that went down on the "504 Conversation for Success" form. Naturally, such a statement would not instantly take care of the negative relationship with the student because the student needed to also take part in the collaboration, but what I ultimately found with each student who disliked his teacher was a need to be accepted by that teacher. Together, the student and I would brainstorm more interventions, using the question "What can you begin to do to show Ms. King that you can be a good student? What would she say you could do?"

Then, framing the intervention as an experiment, the student and I would visit Ms. King personally (I did this for each teacher whose relationship with

504 Conversation for Success

Date: _____

Student: _____   Grade: _____

Attendees:

_____

_____

Primary concern:

_____

Miracle question: Suppose tomorrow when you return to school, things have changed so that you have a good day. What will be different then? Who will do things differently during that day, including you and your teachers?

_____

_____

_____

_____

What difference will that make for you?

_____

_____

_____

Exceptions—Tell me about times when some of your ideas have occurred in the past:

_____

_____

_____

_____

_____

Let's develop some strategies for you and your teachers, based on your ideas:

_____

_____

_____

_____

Student: _____   504 committee chair: _____

504 Meeting Summary for Teachers—Sample

Date: 5-10-10

Student: Jeremy S.   Grade: 4

Dear Teachers,

Jeremy S. has identified what would help him to be more successful at school. Please talk briefly with the student about his ideas and try out these strategies for the next three weeks with him.

1. It helps me when the teacher asks me whether I understand the assignment before going on to another topic. I am shy, so I don't always ask.
2. If a teacher shows me how to study for a test, I am less anxious and I do better.
3. I do better when I work in a group.
4. I learn best in a quiet area away from friends.
5. I stay on track when another student who knows the assignment works with me.
6. Sometimes I need one extra day to finish an assignment.

Please comment about what seems to be helpful for this student and return this sheet to the 504 committee chair in three weeks.

What's working:

_____

_____

_____

_____

_____

_____

_____

Teacher Signature

504 Meeting Summary for Teachers

Date: _____

Student: _____   Grade: _____

Dear Teachers,

_____ has identified what would help him or her to be more successful at school. Please talk briefly with the student about his or her ideas and try out these strategies for the next three weeks with him or her.

504 committee chair _____   Student _____

Student Strategies

Please comment about what seems to be helpful for this student and return this sheet to the 504 committee chair in three weeks.

What's working:

_____

_____

_____

_____

_____

_____

_____
Teacher Signature

a student was not productive) and very briefly announce to the teacher that her student had designed some new strategies for learning or behaving better in her class. This type of visit typically resulted in much less resistance on the part of the teacher, who had often been burned by the student, and in the student, who now had committed to trying something new.

Chapter Perspectives to Consider

Can an RTI process be this simple? Yes. A solution-focused process may lead to interactions like these:

- Showing interest and curiosity about how a single mother with two jobs and five kids at home can accomplish so much might result in an empowering conversation in which she feels understood, making it more likely that she will reinforce the importance of school with her children.

  "Ms. Kerr, I recognize the enormous responsibilities you have, working so much and caring for five children. I have to say that I am very impressed. I don't know how you do it all. You obviously know what is important. I wonder if you might consider . . ."

- Talking honestly with your colleague, who has fewer issues with Juan than you do, and asking what he does that you might try with Juan in order to create change in your classroom, will boost your relationship not only with the colleague but possibly with Juan.

  "Larry, can you help me with something? I notice that Juan seems very engaged in your science classroom. What is it that you have found to engage him?"

- Complimenting instead of punishing a student who is off task or forgets to do homework because she cares for her three younger siblings at night will place responsibility back on the student in a way that makes her feel understood rather than alienated and may lead to her trying harder to complete her work.

"Carrie, I realize that you have to look after your brother and sisters while your mom works at night. I have to say I am very impressed with your responsibility. I wonder how you might use that sense of responsibility to begin doing some of your schoolwork. I would also like to know how I, as your teacher, can assist you."

- When a student begins losing enthusiasm for school in March, remembering that she did well in the fall semester instead of speculating on what happened that made her fail would lead you to wonder what was working in the fall semester. Irrespective of the fact that her family life did change in the spring, just talking to the student about what worked will change her view of you as her teacher and may lead to a more compliant student.

"Shari, you are a remarkable young girl. I know you have been through a lot lately with your family, yet I also recall how success-ful you were in the fall. Can we talk about what I might have done and what you might have done then that worked for you?"

Chapter 6

Parent Conferences That Collaborate Instead of Intimidate: Level A

Who would wants to answer a phone call from the school when the assumption is that something else is wrong with Johnny? Who would want to attend a meeting in which problems are the primary focus, even though the teachers present say that they like the student? Many parents are stressed with work and financial responsibilities, so another problem at school may be low on their priority list. Typically, parents are called when a referral for RTI is made and told that there will be a meeting on a certain date and that their attendance will be important as a plan is made. Gee, how inviting! Many parents don't show up, leaving the team members to decide on their own what is best for the student, who is also not present. When the strategies don't work later, the teacher or team often blames such failure on lack of parental support for the team, the teacher, or the student.

How parents are invited to RTI meetings is vital for their attendance.

Later sections of this book will offer more discussion on how to deal with parents who are reluctant to get involved at school meetings. Until then, consider the importance of recognizing parents as the real experts on their own child. Consider carefully how you phrase your invitation for them to attend the next RTI team meeting, whether it is through a phone call or a written note. A note might be worded like this:

Ms. Lopez, on Monday afternoon at 4:30, Jose's team of teachers and I are going to gather to discuss some things that can make his school experience better for him. Because you are his mother, we consider you an expert on Jose. Would you please join us on Monday? We would welcome and appreciate your participation, because you know Jose best and we want you, along with Jose, to help us develop some new plans for him. Until then, would you think of ways that other teachers have been helpful to Jose? Your observations are valuable to us.

Respectfully,
Hector Vega
Team A, Howard Elementary School

The odds of her showing up just increased greatly. Wouldn't you go if you were considered the expert on your child?

In 2004, I helped to develop a program for Davenport Community Schools in Davenport, Iowa, which began with a conversation among students, parents, and teachers about their concerns. The district was experiencing an overabundance of referrals to special education, and district administrators wanted not only to decrease the number of referrals but also to improve staff and student morale. Three types of intervention conversations were developed, and the first type, Level A, will be discussed in this chapter as the first step in a Tier II intervention. Through Level A conversations, strategies for student success were rapidly developed, resulting in a drastic decrease in special education referrals in Davenport. A template for a Level A conversation is shown in the next section.

In each school that undertook the solution-focused RTI process explained in this book, it was agreed that no referral to special education could be made until Level A, B, and C conversations were held. This system placed much more responsibility on parents, students, and teachers, who at first were hesitant to recognize their ability to work in such an innovative way. After many years of using the approach, however, the teachers in Davenport now feel much more competent as educators. With their students' help, they have stretched their creative resources and led students to realize that success can be collaboratively created.

Focus on Solutions: Level A Conversation

Level A intervention begins when teachers, parents, an administrator, or a student express concern about a student's performance. Similar to a routine parent conference, a Level A conversation is held to state the concern, rate current progress on the ten-point scale, state goals, and explore exceptions. Everyone attending the meeting agrees to try out the exceptions that are identified, and the teacher may add research-based curriculum that fits the identified exceptions, if such compatibility occurs. Everyone in the Level A meeting agrees to try out the plan for three weeks. Each week, the student's success is rated on the ten-point scale by both teacher and student, and a log of exceptions and successes is kept. The feedback is shared at the next meeting with the parent and student. If the student's scale score increases, the student stays at Level A. If the student does not move up the scale after three weeks, a Level B meeting is convened for that student.

Solution-Focused RTI Conversation: Level A

Date: _____

Student: _____ Grade: _____

Primary teacher: _____ Team: _____

Attendees (parent, teacher, and student):

_____

_____

1. **Identify hopes:** The teacher opens by expressing appreciation to those attending the meeting, then starts the conversation: *"What are your best hopes for our meeting today?"*

   (It is common for attendees to answer by saying what they do *not* want. Help those who respond in this way to develop a more workable goal by asking, "What do you want to happen instead?")

   Parent: _____

   Student: _____

   Teacher: _____

   "On a scale of 1 to 10, with '1' being not successful and '10' being completely successful, where is the student in regard to what we want to achieve?"

   Parent: _____ Student: _____ Teacher: _____

2. **Set goals:** The teacher thanks the parent and student for their responses and asks, *"What will the student be doing in the classroom over the next three weeks so that the score increases and our concern decreases?"*

   Parent: _____

   _____

   Student: _____

   _____

   Teacher: _____

   _____

3. **Identify exceptions:** The teacher asks about times when behavior or performance as described in the goal occurs or has occurred in school or at home: *"When is this happening or when has it happened slightly already in other classrooms, grades, or situations at school or even outside of school?"*

(continued)

Solution-Focused RTI Conversation: Level A (*Continued*)

Parent: _____

_____

Student: _____

_____

Teacher: _____

_____

4. **Develop strategies:** The teacher, parent, and student then decide which exceptions can be used and adapted in the classroom and at home for the next few weeks.

   Classroom strategies:

   _____

   _____

   Curriculum addition based on exceptions:

   _____

   _____

   Home strategies:

   _____

   _____

5. **Set targets:** The teacher restates the rating scores from the beginning of the conversation and asks the parent and student what scaling they hope the student will achieve by the end of the next week.

   Parent: _____   Student: _____   Teacher: _____

   Summary: The teacher asks the parent and student, *"What was helpful for you today in this conversation?"*

   Parent: _____

   _____

   Student: _____

   _____

   Next meeting date: _____   Time: _____

   _____

Source: Adapted from Metcalf, 2008b.

On the two pages of the "Solution-Focused RTI Conversation: Level A" form, an assessment, strategies, and plans are compiled in a format that is easy to follow. The teacher can make a copy of the Level A conversation, hand it to the parent, and keep a copy in an RTI strategy file; thus, parent and teacher become partners in working for the student's success.

Thereafter, the classroom teacher (or teachers), along with the student, will monitor and document the student's progress toward goals on a weekly basis, using a scale of 1 to 10 in which "10" means completely successful and "1" means minimal or no success.

In addition, over the next three weeks, the teacher (or teachers) watch for exceptions and document them on the "Exception Findings: Level A" form. Because they have so many other students to care for, it is easy for teachers to overlook success; therefore, it is very effective for the teacher to consult the student each week to inquire about what the student saw as success and identify more exceptions. Furthermore, when a student is consulted, he is empowered and motivated to continue showing success, The teacher and student also discuss what score to give the student for each week. This procedure keeps the assessment and documentation current and involves the student, keeping him engaged, all through the use of only a single page! It is a gentle reminder that the teacher has flipped the coin and is looking for exceptions more than problems.

Many teachers have also found that writing a very brief note home to parents whenever possible boosts the development of more exceptions. An example of such a note is shown here:

Dear Parents,

This is a short note to let you know that today, Jose completed his math assignment and turned it in before he left for recess, even though he was rushing out the door! I was quite impressed. Hooray for Jose!

Linda Metcalf

When the follow-up meeting convenes after three weeks, the "Exception Findings: Level A" sheet should be shared with the parent and student. If even the slightest amount of progress has been made, it is assumed that the strategies are working. Together, the meeting participants should then focus on increasing the use of strategies that are working and adding others that have occurred to them. They will then continue to monitor the student's progress and assess progress again in three more weeks. As progress is made, the meetings can be spaced out, with longer intervals between them.

Exception Findings: Level A

Date: _____

Student: _____   Grade: _____

The documentation on this page is *only* for exceptions—times, situations, or activities when the student begins to be more successful in the classroom.

Week 1 Exceptions: List activities, situations, or assignments:

1. _____
2. _____
3. _____
4. _____
5. _____

Weekly score: _____   Student: _____   Teacher: _____

Week 2 Exceptions: List activities, situations, or assignments:

1. _____
2. _____
3. _____
4. _____
5. _____

Weekly score: _____   Student: _____   Teacher: _____

Week 3 Exceptions: List activities, situations, or assignments:

1. _____
2. _____
3. _____
4. _____
5. _____

Weekly score: _____   Student: _____   Teacher: _____

Follow Up After Three Weeks

After three weeks, the teacher, parent (or parents), and student meet again to glance over the "Exception Findings: Level A" form, focusing on what worked during the three weeks. If the student's score increases slightly, the student stays in Tier II, and the Level A conversation continues until a measurement of success that is deemed appropriate is noted by the teacher. A new "Exception Findings" sheet can be used for every three weeks and put into the student's RTI file. Thus, successful strategies that have been noted on the exception sheets are sent on for the next year's teacher to review.

If the student is not successful after two attempts at the Level A meeting, a Level B meeting is convened for the student. Level B meetings are also part of Tier II. In a Level B meeting, parents, the student, all teachers involved in the student's day, a school counselor, and an administrator examine more exceptions.

Chapter Perspectives to Consider

Before referring a student to a Tier II Level A meeting, try conversing with the student, using the conversation template in Chapter Five. Also, try phoning the student's parent and using the template as a basis for a conversation prior to referral. Ask the questions in the template in a genuine and sincere manner, probing for times when school worked better. Hardly a parent or student would balk at inquiries about actual successes.

Don't be surprised if the students or parents you ask are a bit taken back by the solution-focused questions. Like many educators, they may find it difficult to see past concerns toward times when school worked slightly better. Yet once they are in the habit of seeking exceptions rather than concerns, blaming the school will come to a halt and motivation will appear almost magically in students. Don't believe it? The next time a student that you are concerned about is off track, take the student to a private area and say something like this:

> Kate, I am glad you are in my class. I have a concern, though, that I would like to talk to you about. I notice that it is hard for you to turn in your homework sometimes. When I looked at my grade book, I noticed that for three days out of five this week, you turned in your science homework. How did you manage to do that?

Listen for Kate's response. She may reply with a smile and say, "I don't know."

You might respond, "I don't know either! Can you think about what you did and tell me tomorrow?"

With another student, you might say,

Jason, I know it's hard for you to sit in your seat sometimes. I noticed yesterday that you sat in your seat for ten minutes. I was quite impressed. It was during our social studies class. Do you remember? I wonder how you did that, because it certainly helped me!

Listen for Jason's response. He, too, may be surprised that you noticed.

Then, after Jason gives you an answer (or even if he does not know the answer yet), ask him if he can try for ten minutes during science and math.

You will begin to see how small steps lead to big changes.

Chapter 7

The Team Approach in Solution-Focused RTI: Level B

For some teachers, it is puzzling when certain students do slightly better in other classes than they do in theirs. They are good teachers. They provide excellent activities, use visual aids, and reinforce good behavior, yet Sally just doesn't seem to catch on in their class like she does in their colleague's across the hall.

Focus on Solutions: Level B Conversation

A student is referred for a Level B conversation when the student's primary teacher or subject teacher finds that Level A conversations have not been successful. Prior to a Level B meeting, all teachers involved in the student's day as well as the student's parent (or parents) are asked to prepare by collecting exceptions, using the "Exception Observations: Level B" form on the next page.

On the day of the meeting, the student and the student's teachers, administrator, school counselor, and parent (or parents) gather, each bringing their "Exception Observations" form. The leader of the meeting follows the format on the "Solution-Focused RTI Conversation: Level B" form. As the meeting concludes, a copy of the completed "Solution-Focused RTI Conversation: Level B" form is provided to each attendee so that everyone can participate in the strategies. Another meeting is set for three weeks later.

Using the "Exception Findings: Level B" form, the student is rated weekly on a scale of 1 to 10 by her teachers and is asked to rate her own progress as well. Three weeks after the first meeting, a follow-up meeting is held. If the Level B process accomplishes the goals that were set by the team, referral to the next level is unnecessary. If goals are not met within a time frame designated by the team, the student is referred to the next level, Tier III, which involves convening a Level C meeting.

Exception Observations: Level B

Student: _____ Teacher: _____

Dear Teacher,

There will be a solution-focused RTI Level B meeting for _____

_____ on _____

at _____ in room _____. Your presence is

requested because you are an important member in the student's academic life. The meeting will not last longer than thirty minutes.

Prior to the meeting, please notice times when this student is slightly successful in your classroom. Note the kinds of lessons, activities, behavioral interventions, motivational strategies, or other methods that help the student be slightly more successful. These "exceptions" to times when the student is less successful should be listed below. Please list at least five exceptions below, and bring the list to the meeting.

Thank you.

_____

Exceptions:

1. _____

_____

2. _____

_____

3. _____

_____

4. _____

_____

5. _____

_____

Solution-Focused RTI Conversation: Level B

Date: _____

Student: _____ Grade: _____

Primary teacher: _____ Team: _____
Attendees:

_____

_____

1. **Identify hopes:** The leader opens by expressing appreciation to those attending the meeting and then starts the conversation: *"What are your best hopes for our meeting today?"*

   (It is common for attendees to answer by saying what they do *not* want. Help those who respond in this way to develop a more workable goal by asking, "What do you want to happen instead?")

   _____

   _____

   _____

   _____

   _____

   _____

   Parent: _____ Student: _____ Teachers (take average score):

   _____ School counselor: _____

2. **Set goals:** The leader thanks everyone for their responses and asks, *"What will the student be doing in the classroom over the next three weeks so that the score increases and our concern decreases?"*

   "On a scale of 1 to 10, with '1' being not successful and '10' being completely successful, where is the student in regard to what we want to achieve?"

   _____

   _____

   _____

(continued)

Solution-Focused RTI Conversation: Level B (*Continued*)

3. **Identify exceptions:** The leader asks about the exceptions that everyone present was asked to document: *"When is this happening or when has it happened slightly already in other classrooms grades, or situations at school or even outside of school?"*

_____

_____

_____

_____

_____

4. **Develop strategies:** The leader asks the student, teachers, parent, and staff members who are present to decide which exceptions can be used and adapted in the classroom and at home for the next few weeks.

   Classroom strategies:

   _____

   _____

   Curriculum addition based on exceptions:

   _____

   _____

   Home strategies:

   _____

   _____

5. **Scaling progress:** The leader restates the rating scores from the beginning of the conversation and asks the participants what rating they hope the student will achieve by the next meeting.

   Parent: _____   Student: _____   Teachers: _____

   School counselor: _____

   Summary: The teacher asks the parent and student, *"What was helpful for you today in this conversation?"*

   _____

   _____

   Next meeting date: _____   Time: _____

Exception Findings: Level B

Date: _____

Student: _____ Grade: _____

The documentation on this page is *only* for exceptions—times, situations, or activities when the student begins to be more successful in the classroom.

Week 1 Exceptions: List activities, situations, assignments:

1. _____

2. _____

3. _____

4. _____

5. _____

Weekly score: _____ Student: _____ Teacher: _____

Week 2 Exceptions: List activities, situations, or assignments:

1. _____

2. _____

3. _____

4. _____

5. _____

Weekly score: _____ Student: _____ Teacher: _____

Week 3 Exceptions: List activities, situations, or assignments:

1. _____

2. _____

3. _____

4. _____

5. _____

Weekly score: _____ Student: _____ Teacher: _____

More Than a Meeting

Every day in schools, meetings are held in which concerns about students are discussed and strategies are designed to help the student be more successful. Students and parents are then told the outcome of the meeting and what steps the school will take to help the student be more successful. These meetings are definitely done to promote success; however, when the school takes on sole responsibility for being the expert who solves the case, little is accomplished to motivate parents or students.

I have a personal example of how parental input can be helpful in figuring out how best to help a student. When my youngest son, Ryan, was in elementary school, he struggled to get his homework turned in, even when he had completed it. I met with four of his teachers one day and simply said that I knew that in two of his classes, he always turned in his work. Those two teachers smiled and said that they knew Ryan was smart and that he just got distracted when it was time to go to recess or lunch, so they routinely asked him personally to turn in his work prior to leaving the classroom. The other two teachers went on about the importance of making Ryan more responsible. I casually mentioned that learning to be responsible was a terrific goal that I certainly respected. Then I asked how each of them learned to be responsible when they were younger. There was silence in the room for a very long time. Then, one by one, the teachers described making new habits, writing a note to remember, having someone remind them and then reward them when they followed through. None of the answers were consistent with what the two teachers who had complained about Ryan's homework were doing. Together, we all, me included, agreed to remind him more often. I also agreed to set up a reward system at home for a good report from his teachers. Ryan gradually developed better habits.

Being the parent of a distractible child such as Ryan provided me with lots of insight as to how schools treat students who don't fit into the box of education. On one occasion, in second grade, Ryan came home with a paper with a grade of 60. He had failed to complete most of the answers on the paper, resulting in a bad grade. He looked at me and said, "Mom, I will be back in a few minutes."

He went to his room, shut the door and, twenty minutes later, came out with the paper completed. I went over the answers, which were mostly correct, and mused, "How did you do this so quickly?"

He said, "It's easy, Mom, when it's quiet." This gave me new ideas to offer the next time his teacher requested a conference about his difficulty in completing tasks in class. If I had been in a Level B or Level C meeting, my observations of what happened at home when Ryan had quiet surroundings would have been invaluable.

Students as young as Ryan know what can be helpful. Observations as a parent, teacher, and school counselor have taught me that I should never doubt the power of student self-awareness and parental input.

In Davenport Community Schools, when the Level A, B, and C meetings were implemented, parents commented on how they appreciated their children being considered for their strengths rather than their deficits. This systemic inclusion of parents and students resulted in students telling me that they felt liked by their teachers, which motivated them to improve both academically and behaviorally. Naturally, there were students whose grades still needed improving, but when teachers began to hear exceptions from their colleagues and collaborate on how to be helpful to students within the regular general education classroom, they began feeling more competent. More competence led to more confidence and more exceptions, and the referral process stopped at Level B most of the time. The successful interventions meant that many children who would otherwise have been tested for and admitted to special education stayed in the general education classroom. In fact, at one elementary school in Davenport, the year prior to the solution-focused implementation had twenty-five referrals to special education. The next year, after the solution-focused meetings were implemented, the number dropped to two referrals.

Granted, students in need of special education should always be referred when it is deemed, as the mandate for RTI states, that all measures of intervention have been tried. Students who stay in the general education classroom win. They have a better chance of growing academically and socially and feel better about themselves. Students gain confidence as they chart their progress on the ten-point scale each week and see some success. And parents see the school as going above and beyond to be helpful. All of this happens because of a meeting.

Case Example: Leticia

Leticia was a fourth-grade student whose low reading level was a concern for her teachers. I was fortunate to attend a Level B meeting in Davenport on one of my visits to the district.

In the room were seven other educators, including the school counselor, each of Leticia's teachers, an associate principal, and the special education teacher. At one end of the long conference table, Leticia and her grandmother Billee sat together, gazing at the meeting participants, looking a bit worried. Next to them was the school counselor, ready with her laptop, which displayed the template that was used for such meetings. She began the meeting:

> Good morning. Thanks for coming, everyone, I know it's early. I promise to have you all to class before school begins at 8:00. We are happy to have Leticia and her grandmother, who wants us to call her Billee, with us today. We are going to have a solution-focused conversation that we think will help to give us some ideas on helping Leticia move up two grade levels in reading.

This is a Level B meeting, which means that for the past six weeks, Billee, Leticia, and her language arts teacher, Ms. Shoffield, have worked together in a Level A process to raise Leticia's reading level from second grade to fourth grade. While there has been some slow progress, Leticia's teacher is still concerned and wanted us to meet so that the group could discuss additional ways to help Leticia. Everyone in this room knows Leticia. Let's introduce you to her grandmother.

As the meeting continued, the school counselor went over the Level A exceptions that had been identified in a parent conference with Billee, Leticia, and her language arts teacher six weeks ago and then asked the teacher to describe Leticia's current success, using a scale. Her teacher described Leticia as a "4" on a scale of 1 to 10 in which "10" meant being at fourth-grade reading level. Afterward, the school counselor talked about the protocol for the Level B meeting. The meeting took thirty minutes (Metcalf, 2008b, pp. 53–54).

After the Level B meeting had concluded, I spoke with Billee and Leticia as they left the room. I was curious about how they felt the meeting went and wondered whether and how it had been helpful. I asked both of them, "What was it like for you to meet with all of the teachers and staff who are involved with Leticia every day?"

The grandmother answered:

You know, when I was first called, I thought it would be like most conferences I've been to, where you hear what's wrong and what you are going to have to do to make it right. In our case, teachers always thought Leticia was dumb, but like I said today, she is behind in reading because her mother left her in charge of three little siblings younger than her while she went out to deal drugs. Leticia rarely made it to school for the past year until I took her in. But it was very different today. Instead of deciding to just put her in special education, they talked about what my granddaughter was doing right. That's a switch. Everybody needs to hear that once in a while, even me! They each seemed to really be concerned.

Leticia answered:

In my last school I couldn't read books in my grade, either, so I was always going to tutoring or I heard people say that I was always behind, and that made me sad. But today, it felt like everyone in the room liked me. [Metcalf, 2008b, p. 54]

The grandmother and each of Leticia's teachers took a copy of the conversation that described what would be helpful to Leticia. Another Level B meeting would occur in three weeks, and the participants would bring their observations of exceptions, school activities that worked, and any other information that might be helpful to Leticia. After a few meetings, Leticia was able to increase her reading score, using research-based curriculum that fit her needs, based on the exceptions developed in the meeting. She was never referred to special education.

Chapter Perspectives to Consider

Using the solution-focused approach to RTI will result in more than student success; it will result in high staff morale and less stress on teachers. Notice how the process is a collaborative one that puts very little pressure on individual teachers to come up with interventions. Perhaps thinking the following thoughts will be helpful as your school adopts this way of conducting RTI meetings.

- There is always an exception. Some students excel in certain subjects more than other subjects. I need to find out what it is about those subjects and classrooms that work . . . and the student knows the answer.
- When I label a student, I mean well, but it keeps me from seeing the student's successes. As I watch for exceptions, I will redescribe the student in order to help myself see exceptions more clearly.
- Parents see their children as extensions of themselves. Would I want my child to have interventions applied to him (or her) without my understanding? What can I do to promote a parent's insight as helpful to the RTI team?
- I need to look at myself as a teacher and, each day, ask myself and my students, "What did we do today that helped students to understand math? Reading? Social studies?" and so on. When I hear their answers, I need to incorporate the answers into the next week's plans.

Tier III

Intensive Individualized Interventions

When less stringent interventions do not produce the desired outcome, the RTI team—administrators, parent (or parents), student, teachers, and staff members—moves toward performing a solution-focused assessment, combining resources from within a school, including the special education department, and from the education resource center in the district. Support personnel such as school psychologists, consultants, social workers, interventionists, and early childhood specialists are also asked to attend the Level C meeting in order to set goals and determine whether pathology may be keeping the student from succeeding. This meeting will focus slightly more on concerns, yet still rely heavily on exceptions. In addition, elective instructors in music, computer skills, physical education, content mastery, or other disciplines are invited if they experience even the smallest success with the student. Together, the parent, student, and the rest of the team dialogue about what needs to happen for the student to experience more success, and then design strategies for intervention.

Chapter 8

The Solution-Focused Assessment

Seeking Strengths and Abilities at Level C

A real advantage of using the solution-focused RTI process is that during Level A and Level B meetings, information and experience are developed that will provide the groundwork for collaboration between student and parent should a more evaluative assessment be needed. Throughout Level A and B meetings, everyone involved strives to seek exceptions, noting successes at times and relying on the other team members for support. Should a Level C meeting be needed, all of the data collected from Level A and Level B is at a team's fingertips, and both the student and the parent recognize that the school has the student's strengths in mind as a Level C meeting approaches. The climate is that of collaboration, and because so much effort has been made to seek solutions without a formal assessment, rarely does a parent feel pushed into testing.

Requests for additional support services from local education agency staff, special education teachers, school psychologists, parents, or administrators occur in a Level C meeting, which also may address possible referrals for health, hearing, or vision screening; monitoring of developmental milestones; or other monitoring. After such exploration, additional interventions are agreed on through the Level C process, and if progress is obtained, this process continues indefinitely, as long as the team approves. If not, consent for a full evaluation of eligibility for special education services is obtained. Union County Public Schools in North Carolina (ucps.k12.nc.us/forms_manager/documents/DescriptionofTierIII-UCPS.doc) state that Tier III

- Provides additional support from administrative staff
- Assists teachers in gaining new knowledge about the identified concern

- Requires in-depth analysis and assessment and further data collection

- Documents plans and assists with ongoing data collection

- Measures effectiveness of intervention plans

- Assists with decision making and making instructional changes in the classroom

- Determines the need for additional resources

Prior to the Level C meeting, the student's parents and each teacher involved in the student's school day should be given the "Exception Observations: Level C" form (shown in the next section) to complete. It is also helpful to ask the parents to bring a list of medications that the student is taking and records from the student's latest medical examinations, including vision and hearing screenings.

The leader of the Level C meeting should gather the solution-focused RTI conversation notes from Level A and Level B and make copies for the group. A review of what has worked slightly should be summarized by the leader prior to the meeting so the meeting can begin with a commentary based on the student's strengths. The hope for the meeting is to increase academic scores or behavior so that the student will achieve appropriate success.

The Level C meeting goes a bit further in its effort to identify solutions by tapping into more resources; community members, consultants, or representatives of the education service center may be invited to participate. These resourceful people will listen for the concerns, so the leader of the Level C meeting will need to monitor the conversation and keep shifting the focus from the many concerns that may be raised to times when the concerns are less overwhelming.

Focus on What Works

In the Level C meeting, it is wise to not include the student initially. In the first part of the meeting, the dialogue will tend to be more focused on symptoms, so it is usually better to keep the student out of those conversations. When it is time to identify exceptions, the student should be introduced to the group and asked to participate in talking about times when school works better. If the student is shy in front of such a crowd, the student should still remain in the meeting to listen to the strategies that will affect her later.

Exception Observations: Level C

Student: _____ Teacher: _____

Dear Teacher,

There will be a solution-focused RTI Level C meeting for _____

_____ on _____

at _____ in room _____. Your presence is

requested because you are an important member in the student's academic life. The meeting will not last longer than thirty minutes.

Prior to the meeting, please notice times when this student is slightly successful in your classroom. Note the kinds of lessons, activities, behavioral interventions, motivational strategies, or other methods that help the student be slightly more successful. Also note how diet or physician-prescribed medications seem to affect or help the student's learning abilities. Watch for vision and hearing issues, and notice when those issues seem not to interfere with learning. These "exceptions" to times when the student is less successful should be listed below. Please list at least five exceptions below, and bring the list to the meeting.

Thank you.

_____

Exceptions:

1. _____

_____

2. _____

_____

3. _____

_____

4. _____

_____

5. _____

_____

The format for a Level C conversation is outlined on the "Solution-Focused RTI Conversation: Level C" form. The focus of a Level C meeting is the student, who deserves to hear that the people in his school life value him enough to take time to discuss how to help him. He needs to feel empowered, so explaining to the student that he has many assets and abilities will help him become more cooperative when he is asked to participate in new activities. It is important for the leader of the Level C meeting to rely heavily on exceptions during the dialogue, pushing participants to look more closely at the student's actions for clues to solutions. To keep the meeting solution-focused, problem talk and probable prognoses should not be encouraged. Solution-focused RTI meetings should *always* result in teachers, parents, and students leaving with hope.

Should dialogue get into negativity and symptom description that begins to lead the group to a hopeless atmosphere, the leader can say: "Thank you for your explanations and concerns. Let's go back to our meeting purpose: to set goals for the student and identify times when those goals are better achieved. Who has seen some progress with the student over the past three weeks? It can be small progress, such as completing an assignment more successfully or behaving more appropriately in a certain setting." If a member of the team insists on talking about what must happen for the student to succeed, stay respectful and ask the team member to continue to observe when the student accomplishes things slightly, in spite of the need that he sees. It has long been a tenet of the counseling profession that no person can change another person. But what we do know is that when one person changes, there is often a change in another person.

Make the Findings Exceptional

After the Level C meeting, team members will monitor the student's progress, watching for exceptions and recording them on the "Exception Findings: Level C" form. At the end of three weeks, the team meets and discusses the exceptions that they have discovered in addition to any test results that they requested.

Asking the team to watch for exceptions is crucial for Level C success. I recall one elementary student, Maria, who would not complete her science and social studies homework correctly, ever. She either got the page numbers of the assignment in her book wrong or failed to write down which chapter she was supposed to review for a test. She became a counseling client of mine at her parent's request, and we talked about times when she did complete her homework correctly. She said she never failed to do her math or language arts homework correctly; she always got those subjects right. I asked what was different in those classes, and she said she sat near the blackboard—so near that she could almost touch it, she said with

Solution-Focused RTI Conversation: Level C

Date: _____

Student: _____ Grade: _____

Primary teacher: _____ Team: _____

Attendees:

_____

_____

1. **Identify hopes:** The leader opens by expressing appreciation to those attending the meeting, and then starts the conversation: *"What are your best hopes for our meeting today?"*

   (It is common for attendees to answer by saying what they do *not* want. Help those who respond in this way to develop a more workable goal by asking, "What do you want to happen instead?")

   _____

   _____

   _____

   _____

   _____

   _____

   "On a scale of 1 to 10, with '1' being not successful and '10' being completely successful, where is the student in regard to what we want to achieve?"

   Parent: _____ Student: _____ Teachers (take average score):

   _____ School counselor: _____

2. **Set goals:** The leader thanks everyone for their responses and asks, *"What will the student be doing in the classroom over the next three weeks so that the score increases and our concern decreases?"*

   _____

   _____

   _____

(continued)

The Solution-Focused Assessment

Solution-Focused RTI Conversation: Level C (*Continued*)

3. **Identify exceptions:** The leader asks about the exceptions that everyone present was asked to document: *"When is this happening or when has it happened slightly already, in other classrooms, grades, or situations at school or even outside of school?"*

_____

_____

_____

_____

_____

"I will read some successes that were noted in Level A and Level B. Who has found that one of these strategies has assisted in raising the student's weekly rating score?"

_____

_____

_____

"When else in the past has this student been able to increase academic success on a small scale? Was it in tutoring, in group work, with individual help, or something else?"

_____

_____

"What was different or helpful in that situation?"

_____

_____

4. **Develop strategies:** The leader asks the team and parent (or parents), *"Which additional resources do you think might help the student be more successful?"* (some examples: vision screening, hearing screening, developmental milestone assessment)

_____

_____

_____

_____

To resource personnel: *"When could we get some assessment data from you?"*

_____

The leader asks the student, parent, teachers, and staff members who are present to decide which exceptions can be used and adapted in the classroom and at home for the next few weeks while the community resource personnel conduct assessments.

Classroom strategies:

_____

_____

Curriculum addition based on exceptions:

_____

_____

Home strategies:

_____

_____

Summary: The leader asks the teachers, staff members, resource staff members, parent, and student: *"What was helpful for you today in this conversation?"*

_____

_____

_____

_____

Next meeting date: _____ Time: _____

a smile. I asked how that helped, and she told me she could see the board better close up. She said that in the other two classes, she sat in the back and couldn't see the blackboard with the assignment very well.

We got her a vision screening, and sure enough, she desperately needed glasses.

A Solution-Focused IEP

Individualized Education Plans (IEPs) are mandated for students who qualify for special education services under state and federal laws. Typically, IEPs are problem-focused, asking questions about the problem. While focusing on problems is sometimes helpful, when educators are done with their checklists, they must come up with interventions to assist the student. A solution-focused IEP consistently focuses on times when the problem does not occur as often, leading to exception gathering and then solutions.

The solution-focused IEP will be a different kind of experience for educators, as it seeks out not only challenges, but also when those challenges are manageable. The team can then summarize what kind of environment the student performs better in, whether it be a special education classroom or a general education classroom as inclusion or content mastery. Imagine the hope cultivated in such a process! A parent who had the experience in the past of hearing all that is wrong with her child will learn when her child is slightly more successful and will hear it from educators who seek such exceptions diligently.

The "Solution-Focused Individualized Education Plan" shown in this section is meant to be used at Level C meetings if the team deems it would be helpful in pursuing academic strategies and interventions.

Glancing through the IEP form, you will notice that each section seems typical in its dedication to understanding the limitations of the student. However, each section also includes items with a more solution-focused purpose, which are marked with asterisks. After the limitations are stated (which is required by most districts), the solution-focused statement provides information for planning at the end of the meeting. The team will fill out each section of the IEP and then gather the solution-focused answers and compile them into a plan. No extra brainstorming is needed.

Because the solution-focused IEP requires observations of exceptions, more than one meeting may be required to complete it. If team members do not know of any exceptions when they are asked for them in the IEP, it may be helpful to ask them to use the "Exception Observations: Level C" form that is found in Chapter Eight. After the team has met at least twice, they can determine whether to refer the student for a full test administration to determine learning

Exception Findings: Level C

Date: _____

Student: _____ Grade: _____

The documentation on this page is *only* for exceptions—times, situations, or activities when the student begins to be more successful in the classroom.

Week 1 Exceptions: List activities, situations, assignments:

1. _____

2. _____

3. _____

4. _____

5. _____

Weekly score: _____ Student: _____ Teacher: _____

Week 2 Exceptions: List activities, situations, assignments:

1. _____

2. _____

3. _____

4. _____

5. _____

Weekly score: _____ Student: _____ Teacher: _____

Week 3 Exceptions: List activities, situations, assignments:

1. _____

2. _____

3. _____

4. _____

5. _____

Weekly score: _____ Student: _____ Teacher: _____

difficulties and then placement in special education. By the time this determination has been made, the parents have witnessed educators who have observed the student for strengths, adapted lesson plans, and spent hours learning from each other on how best to teach the student. Such work profoundly shows the diligence of the educators and makes transitioning from general education instruction to special education instruction more palatable.

The solution-focused process is about empowerment and creating hope within the lives of students, teachers, and parents. The solution-focused IEP that follows is designed to fulfill district requirements as well as provide insight into classroom management, learning styles, and teaching styles that can make all the difference in a student making progress.

Solution-Focused Individualized Education Plan (IEP)

Date: _____

Student: _____ Grade: _____

A. Physical Competencies

1. Physical requirements that affect participation in instructional settings:

   _____ No physical limitations; no modification of regular class needed

   _____ Some physical limitations; no modification of regular class needed

   _____ Needs modifications because of the following impairment:

   _____

   In what activities does the impairment *not* affect the student or affect the student less? List specific activities:

   _____

   _____

   Describe the modifications needed, based on the listed activities:

   _____

   _____

2. Physical requirements that affect physical education:

   _____ Yes _____ No The student is capable of receiving instruction in the essential elements of physical education through the regular program without modifications.

   If no, list activities in which the student *is* able to receive instruction:

   _____

   _____

   Recommendation, based on competencies in the listed activities:

   _____

   _____

(continued)

Solution-Focused Individualized Education Plan (IEP) (*continued*)

B. Behavioral Competencies

1. Educational placement and programming:

   _____ Student requires no modifications.

   _____ Student has some characteristics that may affect learning, though not severe enough to withdraw from regular classes:

   _____ Poor task completion

   _____ Impulsive—requires reminding to work slowly

   _____ Other: _____

   Abilities that emerge in specific learning tasks or activities and enhance cooperation in the classroom, as identified by teachers, administrators, or parents:

   _____

   _____

   _____

2. Ability to follow disciplinary rules:

   _____ Appropriate for age and cultural group. May be treated the same as non-handicapped student. Student is able to follow the district's discipline management plan. Use of alternative educational placement and suspension per regulations is appropriate. Student is responsible for school board rules and campus policies without modifications.

   _____ This student is responsible for school board rules and campus procedure. A modified discipline plan will be used. The following approaches have been identified as *effective* in working with this student through direct observation by teachers, administrators, or parents:

   _____

   _____

   _____

C. Pre-Vocational or Vocational Competencies

The following skills may be prerequisite to vocational education. Rate each on a scale of 1 to 10 in which "1" = completely unskilled and "10" = completely competent.

_____ Cognitive skills		_____ Communication skills	
_____ Reading level		_____ Organizational skills	
_____ Performance		_____ Social skills	
_____ Verbal comprehension		_____ Following directions	
_____ Attendance		_____ Personal hygiene and self-care	
_____ Punctuality			

Other: _____

Noting all skills with a rating of 6 or higher, list opportunities within the school program that seem appropriate for a student with those competencies:

_____

_____

_____

_____

_____

_____

D. Academic and Developmental Competencies

1. Rate the student's *competence* in each of the following content areas on a scale of 1 to 10 in which "1" = completely unskilled and "10" = completely competent. (Grade or age levels alone are not sufficient.)

_____ All subjects	_____ English	_____ Health
_____ Reading	_____ Science	_____ Vocational skills
_____ Math	_____ Spelling	_____ Fine arts
_____ Social studies	_____ Computer literacy	_____ Physical education

Other: _____

2. List the subject competencies that are scored 6 or higher below, and in collaboration with the assigned teacher, briefly describe the teaching methods that have been identified as *effective* with this student.

Subject   **Effective Teaching Methods**

_____

_____

_____

_____

_____

_____

(continued)

Solution-Focused Individualized Education Plan (IEP) (*continued*)

3. Indicate with a checkmark the content areas in which the student needs more assistance in developing competence and could benefit from a special education program.

_____ All subjects	_____ English	_____ Health
_____ Reading	_____ Science	_____ Vocational skills
_____ Math	_____ Spelling	_____ Fine arts
_____ Social studies	_____ Computer literacy	_____ Physical education

Other: _____

4. List the checked subjects from item 3 in the space below, and match appropriate teaching methods from item 2 that have been proven effective and that might lead to more competent performance.

Subject   **Suggested Teaching Method**

_____

_____

_____

_____

_____

Source: Adapted from Metcalf, 2008b, p. 113.

Chapter Perspectives to Consider

I recently spoke to some young college students at a Gateway to College (GTC) conference about the solution-focused approach that their instructors were learning. The GTC program is a marvelous program that offers students who have dropped out of high school a chance to complete their diploma and two years of community college at the same time. Most of these students have not had warm and fuzzy educational experiences. Most of their parents were told that their kids could not make it in school.

After speaking for a few minutes, I asked the students what they thought about the solution-focused process, particularly the part where students are seen as the experts.

A Hispanic adolescent named Maria raised her hand and said, "I am so glad that they are learning this, because when you are trying to mature like we are, you don't want to listen to people tell you how to fix your life. But if someone asks you what you want and then helps you figure it out, that helps a lot more."

Given that thought, here are some perspectives for you to try out:

- If we all fit into the same box, completing interventions would be easy, but humans won't always follow our rules, because they are ours, not theirs.
- Tommy Hilfiger, Terry Bradshaw, Whoopi Goldberg, and many more famous people didn't fit the mold yet excelled enough to produce ideas and inventions and laughter that keep life interesting.
- What if the child who can't read—yet—or the adolescent who constantly asserts herself inappropriately is destined to be one of the great ones who will feed the hungry or stop global warming? Who are we to say, "You must comply and learn this way"?
- Today, I will listen and watch for exceptions; therein lie solutions for both me and the student.

The next three chapters were written by school counselors who used the solution-focused approach in everyday situations and meetings involving RTI. May their success and excitement be contagious!

Chapter 9

The Exceptional Elementary School

Sarah Switzer

Life is not about waiting for the storms to pass, it's
about learning how to dance in the rain.

Remember the in-service
When you learned of RTI?
It was probably in August,
But you were dreaming of July!
A representative of the ISD
Came to your campus,
To explain when students struggle,
We must increase the chances
For them to be successful
In each and every class,
For when it comes to testing,
Everyone must pass!
We have all heard the story
Of this important test
And how each child must progress
And stay up with the rest.

Now we hear a new name,
Response-to-Intervention.

This must be the answer,
An educational invention!
RTI for short,
Whatever does it mean?
When a student struggles,
We must intervene.

It is neatly dissected
Into three specific parts,
To individualize the program
That increases students' smarts.
These parts we know as tiers
Begin in the classroom,
And with creative teaching
Student ability will bloom.

If they still have trouble,
We can move on to Tier II.
Outside help is required
For the student to pull through.
If the problem is persistent,
Then Tier III is what we need.
Special ed may be suggested
For the student to succeed.

Tier I

This section will explain how Tier 1 interventions appear in the elementary school. There will be questions that ask you to review your current school situation and ideas to help you develop strategies that attempt to meet the needs of all students.

The Sea of Experiences

Let us imagine, for a moment, that our students are self-sufficient vessels, boats if you will, floating in a vast sea of experiences. These boats are equipped with everything needed to navigate the waters, but they are not all the same. Some are enormous yachts with every bell and whistle available, high-tech gadgets to locate and detour around possible stormy seas, and GPS so they never get lost. Others may not be so well equipped, yet still have the basic requirements for aquatic navigation. On this great sea of experience, we find speedboats looking for the fastest path, tugboats that pull way more than their share, battleships always on the lookout for a fight, party barges in search of a good time, sailboats going whichever way the wind blows, rowboats reaching their destination only after a great deal of hard work, lifeboats just working on survival, and even an occasional dinghy (no pun intended) with no real direction or destination just out there floating. Each of these vessels possesses specific advantages that fit them for different experiences, and each student, or captain, is an expert on her own vessel, knowing which tasks come naturally or easily and which are a struggle or a challenge.

The teacher is the wind and current, which meet each student wherever she may be on the vast sea of experiences. Becoming familiar with each vessel and its strengths and helping each captain recognize and utilize these strengths creates an environment for achieving greater possibilities. Only after the teacher joins with each vessel, wherever it is, and becomes a fellow voyager, can he guide it to where it needs to be. The teacher must visit the vessel of his student in order to discover the abilities he never knew the student possessed. This is where Tier I begins.

New Questions

Where do your students excel? What really motivates them? What truly interests each one of them? As an elementary school counselor using the solution-focused approach, I have found that the best way to answer these questions is to ask! Yes, I ask elementary students. There is no magic age at which a child realizes, "Now I am old enough to know what I like and dislike." This feat is accomplished as an infant; the difficult part is communicating those likes and dislikes to others. What a student likes and enjoys usually translates into something they are good at or are at least willing to put extra effort into. These are the first signs of strength. Use them to their full potential. This is what is *right* with that student!

When we help our students become aware of these *exceptions,* times when students are slightly more successful, they are able to create their own solutions to solve problems. This approach works well in the classroom. The key is for the teacher to create an environment in which each student can use his own strengths to be successful in every subject, every time. While this sounds wonderful and amazing, how can a teacher accomplish that and how does it fit with RTI?

Proactive and Preventive

Response to Intervention, Tier I begins in the regular education classroom. The goal of Tier I is to proactively monitor student progress and prevent situations that may lead to learning deficiencies or challenges. Tier I addresses the needs of all students, not just students who receive special education services. Knowing the student's strengths is vital in creating a learning environment conducive to success.

One way to find out about student strengths is to start each school year with a student survey. The survey does not have to be formal; an example is shown in this section. This "Student Survey" form can be reproduced and used at the beginning of the school year as well as periodically throughout the year to track changes in individual students' preferences, learning, and effort. It is also helpful for the students to review this form, offer feedback at the end of the school year, and reflect back on the success and growth they've experienced. When accompanied by sample work or other assessment data, this form can also be used to track progress for RTI requirements.

Written and oral responses to the survey can both be beneficial. The choice of verbal or oral is up to the teacher who knows her students best. The key is to make the questions meaningful and age-appropriate for your students' grade level. At the beginning of a school year, using the survey will give helpful insight into how to meet each student where he or she is. Proactively learning about each student's strengths may help prevent some major behavioral and learning challenges. The survey should reveal specific strengths and interests and serve as a guide for motivating each student. The information can be used when designing the instructional method for introducing new material.

On finishing a major lesson or unit, enlist the expertise of each student to help discover what both you, the teacher, and the student did that helped create successful learning. This feedback will help you to find out what approaches (for example, activities, projects, presentations, collaborations, or methodology) were beneficial to the learning experience. Providing the feedback will reinforce the student's ability and responsibility in regard to his own learning and underscore the importance of active participation in the learning process. A student is an engaged learner when he feels like a part of the process—a beneficial member with important contributions—instead of a product of the process. Fostering this type of engagement creates successful learners.

The most powerful contribution of any form of assessment happens when it is used to discover what worked. In education, we tend to let what didn't work cloud the big picture. Take a new approach, look for what is working, and then do more of that. By focusing on what works and increasing that, we begin, with little or no effort, to eliminate what doesn't work and increase student success. This concept is not new; I am sure you are familiar with the saying, "If it ain't broke, don't fix it!"

Student Survey

Name: _____   Date: _____

Please answer the following questions. You may use additional paper if necessary.

1. What is your favorite subject in school, and why?

   _____

   _____

2. Would you rather hear a story, read a story, or watch the story acted out, as in a play
   or movie?

   _____

3. What do you enjoy the most about your school day? Explain.

   _____

   _____

   _____

4. What do you do for fun outside of school? (hobbies, activities)

   _____

   _____

   _____

5. Tell me about a personal accomplishment that made you proud.

   _____

   _____

   _____

6. Tell me what else you do well.

   _____

   _____

   _____

7. What can I (as your teacher) do to help you be successful?

   _____

   _____

   _____

8. What will you (as the student) do to help yourself be successful?

   _____

   _____

   _____

Tier I in Action

"Maggie" was a third-grade student who had trouble getting her assignments completed and turned in on time. This problem resulted in Maggie having unsatisfactory marks on her report card, which could lead to problems in advancing to the fourth grade if they continued. Maggie was a bright student who was capable of completing her assignments successfully, yet for some reason she was not doing it. This greatly frustrated her teacher, Ms. Brown. One afternoon as the students were working independently, Ms. Brown called Maggie to her desk. Ms. Brown told Maggie that she did not understand why Maggie's test scores were so high but her other assignment grades were mostly zeros.

Ms. Brown: This could cause problems with your going to fourth grade.

Maggie: [looks at the ground]

Ms. Brown: What is different about taking a test that helps you to do so well?

Maggie: I don't know.

Ms. Brown: Well, I can see that you know the material from your test scores, so I know you can do the assignments. What would need to be different so that you complete the assignments and turn them in?

Maggie: I work on the assignments, and I want each one to be perfect, and then I see other students finishing before me and turning in the assignment. Then I get worried because I am not finished and others are, and so I can't get my work done.

Ms. Brown: Okay, so you are able to do the assignments, but then have trouble when you see others getting finished before you; is this right?

Maggie: Yes, I feel like I should be finished, too.

Ms. Brown: All students work at different speeds, and that is okay. What could be done so that if another student finishes before you, it would not distract you from completing your work?

Maggie: I see them in front of me getting up to turn in the work. If I didn't see that, I could finish.

Ms. Brown: Where could you be so that you would not be able to see all of the other students?

Maggie: I could move closer to the front, so that they would be behind me, or I could go sit in the Reading Room [a somewhat isolated corner of the room that housed the independent reading center].

Ms. Brown: Okay, let's give that a try.

Maggie moved her desk that afternoon before school ended. The next morning, Maggie sat in the front of the classroom. When Ms. Brown finished instruction, the students began independent practice. Maggie began her work and was able to complete the assignment and turn it in without worrying that others had finished before she did. This was successful for the next few weeks, and Maggie was very happy that her idea to sit up front was working so well. A few days later, while the class was working, a boy sitting behind Maggie got up to put his completed work in the tray. As he stood up from his desk, the chair tumbled backward, hitting another desk. The students all turned to look in response to the noise. Maggie saw that the boy was finished and began to frown. Ms. Brown caught Maggie's eye and gave a quick look in the direction of the Reading Room. Maggie smiled, got her things, and finished the assignment in the corner of the room. As the school year proceeded, Maggie had less and less trouble when others finished before she did. She was completing her assignments and feeling good about solving her own problem.

"Collier" was a fourth-grade student who loved to draw. His teacher, Mr. Phish, was concerned because Collier struggled with writing assignments. In fact, Collier usually drew during writing time. Mr. Phish constantly redirected Collier to the task at hand, and usually, Collier responded, "Okay" or "I'm about to start, Mr. P." Collier would write a word or two and then get back to drawing. Mr. Phish was at a loss about how to reach this student, who seemed to have no interest in writing. Mr. Phish decided to bargain with Collier; if Collier did his writing assignment, then he could draw. Collier began to complete writing assignments and turn in his work. Mr. Phish was happy that Collier was producing work, but the quality of the work was poor and did not meet fourth-grade writing expectations.

One day, Mr. Phish saw a finished drawing that Collier had been working on during writing time. Mr. Phish called Collier to his desk to discuss what could be done to help Collier be a successful writer, and he asked Collier to bring the drawing (of which Collier was extremely proud).

Mr. Phish:	I see you have completed your drawing.
Collier [beaming]:	Yes!
Mr. Phish:	You know that you are supposed to be writing an essay now.
Collier [his smile turning to a frown]:	I know, Mr. P, but writing is so boring and I love to draw. I'm pretty good at it, right? [shows the drawing to Mr. Phish]
Mr. Phish:	Yes, you are very talented. What do you enjoy so much about drawing?

Collier:	I can create anything I want. I have all these colors and pictures in my head, and when I start drawing, I know exactly what to draw next. It's easy.
Mr. Phish:	You know, Collier, writing is a bit like drawing, but you use words instead of pictures.
Collier:	It's not the same. Drawing is fun, and writing is boring. When I try to write, I get stuck and don't know what to put. Then I just stare at the page, and all I can think about is drawing something to fill up the space.

Seeing a possible connection, Mr. Phish had an idea. "Collier, tell me about this drawing," he said.

Collier described his drawing in great detail. He described what he was thinking of when he started it and how he chose the colors and shapes for each part of the masterpiece. As Collier described his artwork, Mr. Phish wrote down a few notes.

Mr. Phish [showing Collier the notes]:	Collier, look at all of this information you were able to give me about your drawing. If you wanted other people to understand this picture like you have just explained it to me, how could you do that if the people were not here to listen to your description?
Collier [half grinning]:	Well, Mr. P, I guess I would have to write it down.
Mr. Phish:	That is a wonderful idea, Collier. Get started!

Collier wrote a wonderful essay about his drawing and began to add more detail to his writing assignments. He could still draw after his work was complete, and Mr. Phish was able to incorporate Collier's artistic talents in other areas. Collier now refers to his drawings as "my inspiration." Because focusing on Collier's interests and talents worked so well, Mr. Phish now uses this approach with other students. He has minimal discipline problems, and his students attain remarkable achievement scores.

Teachers who begin using the solution-focused approach to RTI often find that their students provide excellent feedback on their classroom assignments, activities, and programs. The "Learning Feedback" form on the next page can be altered by the teacher for each grade level's reading ability in elementary school.

Tier II

Some students may still have difficulties after Tier I intervention. After strengths have been discovered and incorporated into instruction, a student may still be

Learning Feedback

Name (optional): _____   Date: _____

Please answer the following questions. You may use additional paper if necessary.

Lesson or unit: _____

1. What about this lesson or unit do you remember best?

   _____

2. What did we do in class that really helped you to understand the information?

   _____

   _____

3. What can I as your teacher do more of that would help you continue to be successful?

   _____

   _____

   _____

4. What can you as a student do more of that would help you continue to be successful?

   _____

   _____

   _____

5. On a scale of 1 to 5 (1 = not at all; 5 = very well), how would you rank your understanding of this lesson? Please circle one.

   1 = Did not understand
   2 = Understood some
   3 = Understood half
   4 = Understand almost all
   5 = Understood everything

6. On a scale of 1 to 5 (1 = none; 5 = all), how much effort did you put into learning this lesson? Please circle one.

   1 = none
   2 = some
   3 = half
   4 = almost all
   5 = all

having problems with learning concepts or information or with completing tasks. The teacher will review the student's grades, which may show the student continues to struggle. After such review, the teacher may explore with her colleagues what they are doing in the classroom that may be working for the student. This can be accomplished by simply visiting other colleagues in their classroom or in a more formal setting such as the monthly Student Intervention Team (SIT) meeting. Most SIT meetings are problem focused, so the solution-focused RTI meeting focuses on discussing exceptions that can then be used by the teacher in the classroom. Additionally, in order to determine whether the student may need Tier II support in the future, the team can try additional exceptions and then determine in three weeks if success has been achieved.

The solution-focused RTI tiers should be fluid so that a student can move between the tiers as needed. For example, just because a student is serviced at Tier II, it doesn't mean that she will remain there indefinitely, but the support will always be available to be used as necessary. Imagine a continuum of services that constitute RTI's instructional and behavior support. A student can move along this RTI continuum, and as the student masters objectives, she can move from Tier III, Tier II, or Tier I back toward regular instruction. When Level A and Level B meetings are held, the teachers can decide which exceptions to continue to reinforce. If there is difficulty, the student will move along the continuum of increasing support from regular instruction to Tier I, then Tier II, and, possibly, Tier III.

Tier II interventions are provided in addition to regular core instruction. Ideally, Tier II interventions take place with an interventionist at a separate designated time that does not interfere with or remove the student from regular core instruction. The interventions are based on strategies developed at Level A and Level B meetings, in which exceptions are identified. A minimum of thirty minutes specifically for the purpose of Tier II intervention is scheduled into each day. Making Tier II a scheduled part of the day has more benefits than just meeting RTI requirements. Because the intervention is worked into the general schedule, this time can also be used for additional pull-out programs (for example, gifted and talented, dyslexia, resource, student council, counseling, additional center time, accelerated reading) and still not interfere with instruction time. This can be done on an individual basis with the student's teacher who can best determine which times of the day are best to pull out the student for Tier II instruction. The importance of such collaboration is multifold, as the teacher becomes more likely to try Tier II interventions when she is consulted as an expert.

Tier II In Action

"Abby" is a fifth-grade student who reads at grade level but struggles with math. She loves to read and does so as much as she can. She reports, "Math is just a bunch of numbers that don't make much sense to me." She would much rather read a story that she "can get involved in."

Abby's teacher, Mr. Tuttle, was concerned about Abby's low achievement in math. He chatted with Abby to find out what it was about reading that helped her to be successful.

Abby:	I like finding out what happens next [to the people in her books] and what they will do [in response to different situations].
Mr. Tuttle:	Have you ever read your math book?
Abby:	No, it's just a bunch of numbers.
Mr. Tuttle:	At the beginning of each lesson, there is an explanation that is written out, to help you understand how to do the problems.
Abby:	Oh.
Mr. Tuttle:	Do you think this may help you?
Abby:	Maybe.
Mr. Tuttle:	Are you willing to try it?
Abby:	Sure.

Abby read the explanations at the beginning of the lesson and they made math a little "less boring," but she still struggled with the concepts. Mr. Tuttle and Abby chatted again to see what else could be done to help Abby to be successful in math.

Abby:	I like doing those word problems a lot better than just the number ones. They have a story with them.
Mr. Tuttle:	I can give you some extra word problems that go along with each lesson. Would that help?
Abby:	I don't know; maybe.
Mr. Tuttle:	Are you willing to try it?
Abby:	Sure.

Abby continued to read her math book and work on the additional word problems, but she still struggled. Mr. Tuttle brought Abby's folder to the next SIT meeting, and the team recommended Abby for Tier II intervention. Abby began meeting with the math specialist during the scheduled intervention time for forty minutes each day. With this additional support and continuing Tier I support, Abby made significant progress in math. Now she is working on grade-level math and meets with the math specialist less frequently. She is successful and now needs additional support only periodically. As Abby continues to progress, it will be very helpful for her to complete the "Learning Feedback" form, for it will inform her teachers in upcoming school years about what works for her in learning math.

Tier III

When a student continues to struggle, even with Tier I and Tier II intervention, he may require Tier III intervention. Tier III provides more individualized support for students in need of assistance. One way to achieve this type of support is through before-school or after-school tutoring (or both). Again, this would be a designated time scheduled for intervention. However, in this example, Tier III intervention is scheduled outside of the normal school day, to allow a more individual approach with a smaller interventionist-to-student ratio. It is recommended that the intervention time be set in thirty-minute increments at minimum.

Like Tier I and Tier II, Tier III is not a permanent placement. All three tiers have permeable borders that can be crossed when necessary to meet the needs of the student. It should be possible for a student to transition from regular instruction through the three tier levels and back to regular instruction. It should also be possible for a student to receive additional help in multiple subject areas, if needed, or in just one subject area.

Solution-focused RTI is tailored to each individual student's needs, which means that a student may have different intervention programs to meet her specific needs, based on the exceptions identified in team meetings that included the student and parent. On completion of a Tier III Level C meeting, strategy development, and trial of three weeks, if a student continues to have difficulty progressing, the committee may refer the student for a 504 plan, special education, or another appropriate program offered by the district. If the student is able to be successful with intervention, she will continue to receive the tiered support at whatever level the committee deems appropriate after assessment and evaluation. The student can move between tiers throughout the course of the school year. See the sample "RTI Documentation" forms that provide documentation gathering opportunities to scale success.

Tier III in Action

"Luke" was an extremely energetic and very intelligent second-grade student. He was creative and asked many questions, often interrupting his teacher, Mrs. Basil, as she was instructing the class. He struggled a little with reading, complaining,

RTI Documentation: Tier I Intervention

Date: _____

Student: _____   Grade: _____   Homeroom: _____

	Date	Areas for Tier I Intervention	Student's Strengths	Interventionist	Minutes per Day	Methods	Solutions Discovered	Assessment 1 = Needs intervention; 2 = Making progress; 3 = Mastered
Week:								
Week:								
Week:								

Recommendations: _____

_____

_____

Student will receive: _____ Regular instruction _____ Tier I Tier II _____ (Circle appropriate level of intervention.)

Student will / will not (circle one) be re-assessed in _____ weeks.

Completed by _____   Date: _____

RTI Documentation: Tier II Intervention

Date: _____

Student: _____ Grade: _____ Homeroom: _____

Date	Areas for Tier II Intervention	Student's Strengths	Interventionist	Minutes per Day	Methods and Programs (Research-Based)	Solutions Discovered	Assessment 1 = Needs intervention; 2 = Making progress; 3 = Mastered
Week:							
Week:							
Week:							

Recommendations: _____

_____

_____

Student will receive: _____ Tier I Tier II _____ (Circle appropriate level of intervention.)

Student will / will not (circle one) be re-assessed in _____ weeks.

Completed by _____ Date: _____

RTI Documentation: Tier III Intervention

Date: _____

Student: _____   Grade: _____   Homeroom: _____

Date	Areas for Tier III Intervention	Student's Strengths	Interventionist	Minutes per Day	Methods and Programs (Research-Based)	Solutions Discovered	Assessment 1 = Needs intervention; 2 = Making progress; 3 = Mastered
Week:							
Week:							
Week:							

Recommendations: _____

_____

_____

Student will receive: _____ Tier I   Tier II _____ Referral to _____ (Circle appropriate level of intervention.)

Student will / will not (circle one) be re-assessed in _____ weeks.

Completed by _____   Date: _____

"Silent reading time isn't fun." Luke usually completed assignments that he enjoyed very quickly and was always in need of a new assignment on which to expend his vast supply of energy. However, he had little motivation to complete reading assignments that he saw as boring. When Luke had unstructured time, his excessive energy caused him to get into trouble. When he was not fully engaged or got stuck on a task, Luke complained, "I don't like this" and usually needed frequent reminders to stay on task. He got frustrated easily when situations did not go as he wanted or when he had to stop a project before its completion. His behavior was causing Luke to need additional reading support in the classroom in order to help him continue to progress. Mrs. Basil implemented a reward system for Luke in which he earned tickets when she caught him controlling his energy and behaviors. When Luke earned his ticket, he received additional center time (which he really enjoyed) that he could use after his work was completed and while other students were finishing. This reward system helped Luke to be successful for the next three weeks.

Still, Luke began to have more difficulty during silent reading time. He did not want to read and was having trouble with learning and remembering the new sight words. His behavior began to worsen, and he would not complete the reading assignments in order to receive his tickets as he had before. Mrs. Basil worked with Luke to try to find a strategy that would help him improve his reading, but he still struggled. He was falling behind, so the Student Intervention Team (SIT) recommended him for Tier II intervention. He spent forty minutes with the reading specialist during the scheduled intervention time. At his first assessment after three weeks, Luke had not made progress and was in need of additional support. The SIT recommended him for Tier III intervention.

Luke began to work after school with the reading specialist, using a program in which he listened to headphones as a book was read; he followed along with the recording, seeing each word as he heard it. He then had the opportunity to read the book aloud and work with the computer program to reinforce comprehension. Luke enjoyed this much more, stating, "It wasn't boring, because I was doing something." He developed stronger reading skills and continued to receive Tier I, Tier II, and Tier III support. He made progress with the additional support and was reading on grade level at the last evaluation. The exception of a process of learning that was not boring was extended by using the headphones. How Luke learned best was utilized, and it worked.

Chapter Perspectives to Consider

Most students who need additional help in achieving academic success are identified in the elementary school. By using the solution-focused approach described in this chapter, teachers have the opportunity to turn such identification into a productive process that cultivates hope and growth rather than a process of referral to special education.

The approach described in this chapter shows how a solution-focused approach to RTI can be more productive than a problem-focused approach in that it solicits ideas from students, teachers, and parents themselves. In Chapter Two, the reader had access to stories of successful people who also described the misery they experienced as children with different needs from their peers. Yet the same people went on to be successful in many different ways. What was it that assisted them on such a successful journey? Most of the time it was a parent, teacher, or friend who saw more than a deficit—they saw talent, ability, and competency.

It is the author's hope that if you work in an elementary school that you see the possibilities of a solution-focused approach on the life of a student, her family, and your school. As in the beginning of this chapter, the analogy of a boat with a variety of tools is at your disposal in the form of exceptions. Use them and set sail.

Sarah Switzer, MSSC, a special education counselor in a school district in Texas, uses solution-focused therapy and narrative therapy with students in preschool through twelfth grade. She believes that each student is capable of solving his or her own problems but may become stuck from time to time, forgetting that he or she already knows what to do to be successful. She holds a Bachelor of Arts degree from Texas Christian University and a Master of Science degree in school counseling from Texas Wesleyan University.

Chapter 10

Intermediate School Solutions

Steps to the Future

Patti Gatlin

At the sound of the first bell each day, over 1,000 students hop from buses and cars and scramble up the walkway to our intermediate school. Teachers and administrators greet groups of students as they squish between each other, backpacks swaying and sometimes clashing against one another, as they scurry down the hall to the cafeteria or their team area to begin their day. On the first day of school, their packs are very light, but by the end of the year, a student's backpack is more like a museum of what went on during the year, including, perhaps, some school announcements that never quite made it home!

There are also some invisible things that we could say are zippered inside those backpacks on the first day of the year—things like courage, hope, confidence, enthusiasm, fear, worry, attention difficulties, and talents. Most students' packs are light with hope and anticipation about what they and their friends have imagined about the year ahead, but not all. Some students—fewer in number—carry packs that feel somewhat heavier and contain concerns about having friends, getting good grades, whether the teacher will like them, whether they will be able to stay out of trouble, whether everything will be okay at home while they are at school, or whether they will be able to pass the state assessment that everyone says will be really hard in fifth grade.

The students with the heavy packs filled with discouraging memories of school carry fewer useful tools in their pack. They know that they are supposed to behave and do their work, but sometimes one or both of those things are hard to do. They reach into their pack for a useful tool to help them get motivated, but it's not there. They wear the zipper out on their pack looking for that tool, the ultimate tool that must be in there somewhere. *If I have four dozen pencils and my own ruler in my pack, will I be considered "tooled up" for learning?* they wonder. Not so. This is because the ultimate tool, the one that helps you move ahead, isn't something that can be bought or even taught. It is something that is *believed*. The ultimate tool is within the hidden curriculum, and as counselors, it is our job to uncover the mystery of it and find some spare tools for those students with the heavy packs.

Invisible Problems at Work

Much of the school counselor's work focuses on student problems that are often invisible until the impact of those problems disrupts a classroom or reveals itself through a veil of low performance. One of the really great things about the Response-to-Intervention process for the school counselor is the light that it sheds on these sometimes invisible problems. The conversations that take place during RTI meetings provide clues that provoke questions related to a student's social-emotional struggles, which otherwise would sometimes be difficult to see. Details about academic or behavior struggles and recounting of classroom interactions from several perspectives and within various contexts are useful information that can help the counselor more effectively assist a student who is having difficulty. In addition, the conversations with grade-level teams are like a pulse check for a grade level's guidance needs. When solution-focused questions are added to an RTI process that is already implemented, the questions uncover more things, such as invisible assets.

Transition Years

Fifth and sixth grade are both transition years for students who are in intermediate schools. Fifth-grade students are transitioning in from elementary school, and sixth-grade students are transitioning out to middle school. The first six weeks of fifth grade are very challenging for our fifth-grade students, and the last six weeks of sixth grade are somewhat unsettling for our sixth graders. You might say that the transitional angst seesaws from one section of the building to the next at midyear. The fifth graders and sixth graders express their uneasiness differently. The fifth graders may complain or worry about how they are doing, and sometimes the parents cry, too, whereas the sixth graders in the spring suddenly become aware that they are bigger and that they can be louder, which they surmise means that they are more powerful, and you begin to hear comments from the adults about the fact that it is time to promote them! I wish the adults could have a chance to see those same sixth graders entering middle school as seventh graders. I made the transition with one of my groups one year and was quite surprised to see how meekly they entered the middle school building at the beginning of the year!

The transition from elementary school to intermediate school is a huge event for our fifth-grade students and may be even bigger for their parents. When they first enter the building, parents are startled by its size and by the style of the classrooms. The furniture is larger; there is a gym that resembles the gym that parents remember from high school; and the science labs are designed like laboratories instead of elementary school science classrooms. The students' eyes widen with excitement when they tour the building, but the parents start quivering and glancing nervously at their child and begin checking to see when they can come to see the counselor! When parents visit the team areas, meet the teachers, and see that their child will spend most of the day in a small area of the building with the rest of their team, you can see the relief spread across their faces. Excitement builds when they learn about all the opportunities that students will have for clubs, performances, band, choir, technology training, and fun team sports days.

At the beginning of the year, when parents receive their child's schedule and see its A-B day structure, anxiety peaks again. "Explain this to me," they say.

Their son or daughter usually chimes, "Mom, see, we use this side one day and follow the other side of the schedule the next!" The students have usually already sought out a primary source—an older student—to find out how the schedule works. I see this as evidence that students are wired to find solutions; it is a natural act for them. No wonder our job is so much fun!

In addition to differences in the size and structure of the program, there is a significant increase in the difficulty level of the core curriculum as students move from elementary school to intermediate school. The difficulty continues to increase in the sixth grade, which is the first year that students are issued textbooks that were published by secondary school publishers. Pre-AP courses are offered in the core classes beginning in the fifth grade, and because this is all new territory for students and their family members, the decisions at the beginning of the year about whether to take one or more pre-AP classes are hard to make. And as if all of the transitions and decisions aren't enough for students and parents to deal with, the state testing system has targeted fifth grade as an accountability year for the Texas Assessment of Knowledge and Skills (TAKS), which means that if students do not pass the reading and math assessments, it is likely that they will not be promoted to the next grade. Considering all of these factors, if education was agriculture and Tier I referrals were being harvested, the intermediate school structure would guarantee a bumper crop of RTI from year to year!

The School Counselor and Tier I

A person might say that an intermediate school counselor's role in Tier I RTI resembles a kind of thermostat. A thermostat regulates the temperature so that people are not distracted by a temperature that is too hot or too cold, and intermediate students many times find themselves in these kinds of situations. Neither is comforting or reassuring. A girl who has an argument with a friend, a boy who loses his temper in PE, a student whose grandmother passed away, a child who had an argument with a parent prior to coming to school—these are examples of Tier I concerns, given that each will affect the student's day at school. Friendship problems, homework monitoring, grief, divorce, anxiety, grades, problems in class, social skills in and out of the classroom, time management, anger management, and so on—these and many more would fall under the Tier I umbrella, provided that the counseling occurs in response to a need that arises during the school day. Tier I counseling is the bulk of a counselor's day and year.

Tier I counseling that occurs at the beginning of the school year is often connected with stress and anxiety. Some students find the start of school to be stressful. It is a break in what has been their routine, and sometimes they balk at having to separate from their parents. We might think that by the time students enter intermediate school, anxiety about separating from their parents would be almost nonexistent, but usually, there are a few students who need a little extra support to get their day off to a good start.

Kaci

Kaci was a quiet, gentle, small-built fifth-grade girl who carried a large pink book bag that was about half her height in size. Each morning, her mother would bring her to school. Kaci's bright, sparkling eyes would flood with tears at the point that she and her mom said their good-byes. Crumbling, her mom would bring her to the office, teary, too, at seeing her daughter so sad.

The first week of school, I greeted Kaci with as much energy as I could muster and congratulated her on getting so far inside the door. I was curious about her courage! I told her that it took lots of courage to keep moving forward like that and not to worry about those tears she was shedding. I asked whether I could walk with her and her mom to her class. Kaci's mom looked relieved, and Kaci looked like she wasn't sure that things were going all that well and wasn't too hopeful that things would be improving anytime soon.

I excitedly told Kaci that I had discovered that one of the fun things about coming to a school with so many students was that everyone is different. We all respond differently to things that are new to us. I told her not to be embarrassed that she was feeling sad or that maybe she would shed a tear, because everyone sheds tears from time to time. I was attempting to normalize her behavior, something that the solution-focused approach endorses as a means of helping students to relax and feel normal. Because that seemed to work for Kaci, I did the same the next morning. She started her day with me, and we walked together to her class and talked about the progress she was making. Then we laughed. Around the third day, I began meeting Kaci just inside the door and her mom would say a quick good-bye and leave for work. The tears would well up in Kaci's eyes, but we would chat the tears back. That was the difference that made the difference for Kaci. Her first block teacher would be on the lookout for her and would greet her happily and move her quickly toward her group.

Toward the end of the second week, I began to use the rating question to focus our "walk and talk" on the way to class. I would say, "Kaci, tell me. When you think about how upset and nervous you are right now, on a scale of 1 to 10, with '10' being as upset as you could possibly be, what number would you pick to describe where you are right now?" Kaci would thoughtfully reflect about the question and then give a number somewhere in the middle. (I think the first time we did this, she picked "7.") The first time I asked her this question, I also asked her to tell me the number she would have picked the week before, which would have been the first week of school. When she firmly stated that it would be a "10," I pointed out that she had already made amazing progress. I asked her what her secret was, and she said that she had been keeping her mind set on seeing her friends the minute she entered the room. I mentioned to her that if she were able to walk directly to the room after the bell rang, she would have even more time to socialize with her friends. I also told her that when she was ready for that, she would know it and probably would feel like she had climbed to the top of a very tall mountain! We laughed.

A week or so later, in the morning before school, I was in the library, completing some schedule changes for a couple of students, and Kaci came in, looking nervous and teary-eyed. I asked her to sit next to me for a minute so that I could complete the last schedule with the student who had been waiting. The student, Andy, was also a fifth-grade student, although he was on a different team from Kaci. I didn't know that Andy had experienced separation problems prior to coming to our school.

I introduced Andy and Kaci and mentioned their team names, and Andy said cheerfully, "Oh! Your team is right next to mine! I haven't met you before, though."

Kaci sniffled.

"You know, Kaci, I used to cry, too, when I came to school. It was horrible. I didn't know if I was going to stop or not. I remember everyone looking at me. . . ." When he said that, I began to worry where all of this might go. I held my breath and trusted that everything would not go from bad to worse. The fact was that Andy was often in the assistant principal's office—and not for a reward. Andy continued, "But don't worry. You will feel better. I did, and now I love coming to school!" I thought his last statement was interesting. What a tremendous gift he had for looking on the bright side!

I finished up and gave Andy his schedule. As he was leaving, he turned to Kaci and said, "Nice to meet you! Maybe I'll see you in the hall once in a while."

Kaci had stopped crying, and as we walked to class, I asked her whether it surprised her that another student seemed to understand exactly what she had been feeling.

She said that she had thought that she was the only one who didn't want to leave her mom and that she was acting like a baby.

I reminded her that everyone is different and that every day is a new day. I also told her that no one ever wants to leave their mom! That's normal! In fact, the whole animal kingdom would like to stay with their mom!

That meeting between Andy and Kaci was a turning point for Kaci. She began to come in for our walk less frequently, and eventually, she made it on her own.

Annette

Not all of the students who have difficulty separating are able to settle in as easily as Kaci did that year. Another student, Annette, had challenges from home. Annette's parents were very fearful of school and places outside of their home. Her teachers and I formed a plan that started with my meeting her at her car. Then, a buddy was waiting for her in class, where she and her buddy were given some fun, crafty things to do to help the teacher instead of her going to recess. (Recess was something she didn't like because too many people were running around at once.) We wanted to create an opportunity for Annette to feel competent and confident.

Annette, with her parents' help, had developed a story about school that was not conducive to feeling confidence. Our hope was that school would be so inviting that she wouldn't want to miss it.

Each morning when she arrived, Annette would be in the backseat of the car, sitting next to her mother, and her mother would be holding her tightly, worried that Annette was going to be upset. I asked Annette's mom to take a break and to have her dad bring Annette to school. I told him to drop Annette off at the same place as the other parents who drove their children to school, so that the drop-off wouldn't seem like such a big deal.

Annette's teacher put a welcome sign in her window so that Annette could see it just when the car rounded the corner of the driveway. Instead of pulling over and letting Annette out of the car, her dad parked the car in the lot and waited for the last bell. Annette's attendance became inconsistent. I phoned the family each day that she was absent, and her dad would tell me that Annette was too frightened to go to school. Eventually, after about four months, Annette's family decided to home school her.

My point in telling this story is that although traditional RTI has provided a system for implementing much-needed interventions for students, it has only slightly touched on the role of the family, which greatly affects the effectiveness of the intervention. My second point about this example is that sometimes people become so convinced that a child has a problem that everyone in the family lives by the myth that the problem has a permanent residence in the family. The problem almost becomes more interesting and important than the person, and the focus becomes how to deal with or work around the problem rather than finding a solution that the person can employ so that the person can gain a sense of his own personal strength from being able to solve it. This is very touchy ground for school counselors, depending on how attached the family is to the existence of the problem. If solution-focused RTI had been used with this family and Annette, perhaps the family would have felt less fear and more comradeship with the school. If they had been asked what they wanted for their daughter, they might have noticed the positive atmosphere that is created when a group of teachers, students, and parents come together to discuss competencies.

Focusing on Solutions in the Classroom

The same type of scenario is sometimes played out in classrooms, too. The child may be such a handful for the teacher that instead of formulating a solution, the focus is on managing the problem. I taught in the classroom for over twenty-five years before becoming a school counselor. I know that there were times when I was guilty of putting great energy into finding a way to manage a difficult child. It wasn't that my heart wasn't in the right place. It was just that I truly thought that I could influence behavior by controlling it. I remember replaying events like "he hit the pencil sharpener, pushed a chair, yelled" and spending inordinate amounts of time looking for some kind of point system or something to get the child under control.

What happens when we do that instead of involving the student in the search for a workable solution is that we control the things identified, the child gets a reward, and then the child comes up with a new irritating thing to do. The tables turn on us. Pretty soon the bright child is just cooking up irritations to get another reward! The sad part of situations like I just described is that these methods tend to only validate for the student that he is unable to adapt socially and that everyone, without a doubt, views him as defective.

As school counselors, we can help teachers avoid this kind of trap by letting them in on some of the solution-focused techniques such as the miracle question, the rating question, and the identification of exceptions. The techniques used in solution-focused counseling are a natural fit for the context of the classroom and Tier I. They are also great tools for student work groups to use as topics for a group self-evaluation rubric. The techniques are logical, goal-directed, build self-efficacy, and are devoid of blame and belittling people.

Writing New Life Stories

When students enter our doors, they come to us with their own life story, which has caused them to form generalizations about themselves. Sometimes the stories embody themes of their competence; they know they are good at math or reading or PE. But sometimes the stories they carry are reminders of times when they have failed or looked silly or gotten into trouble. They may hear echoes of people telling them they aren't good at something or that they always do the wrong thing, or they may remember children's voices poking fun or maybe refusing to sit with them at the lunch table, or maybe someone is just looking at them every day like they are just plain weird. This last scenario had been the case with Timothy ever since he had entered school in kindergarten.

Timothy was a fifth-grade student with a K–4 history of behavior problems in school, and he had been described as extremely bright, bizarre, disturbed, and out of control, among other things. His experience at his elementary school was so fraught with discipline issues that his fourth-grade teachers were worried that he would not be able to deal with the structure or the size of the intermediate school campus. The elementary school counselor had a special place in her heart for Timothy, and so she phoned me one morning to invite me over to observe him in class during the spring of his fourth-grade year. I observed him in his class. He kept his face staring down toward his paper. He followed the directions the teacher gave, but he seemed very tense and had no interaction with the other students. As usually happens when we observe students, he did not exhibit the behaviors for which he was so well known. Afterward, I met with the teaching team. They were anxious to let me know how bright he was and that he would need some special attention. They were concerned that he might get lost and overlooked in intermediate school.

When school started the following year, I went to Timothy's team area to see how things were going. Even if I had never seen Timothy before, it would have been easy to spot him in his team area. He walked with his head down and body closed, made little eye contact, and wore his thick, light brown hair at collar length, with the hair on top of his head flowing forward, serving as a shield for his eyes. He carried a book in his hand, and I noticed as the days passed that he would sometimes read it while walking down the hall. Timothy was known as a runner—not the track-and-field kind but the run-from-class-and-hide kind. Timothy and I became acquainted during first block on the first day of school.

I thought a student was crying in the nurse's office, and then I realized it was coming from the assistant principal's office. The crying got louder and louder and then was accompanied by pounding noises. I tapped on the door to see whether I could be of help. The assistant principal invited me in and gestured toward Timothy, who was crouched under a chair, crying—actually more like wailing—and yelling, "No! I am not getting up!" I got down on my knees, lowering myself to Timothy's level. I managed to put my head just outside the chair legs, and for a few minutes, I remained silent and waited. Very soon, he was silent, too. Evidently, his curiosity was awakened, because at this point, he very carefully raised his head just enough to look up through his hair to see whether I was there. That told me two things. One was that he recognized when something didn't fit the norm, and the second was that he wasn't sure how to respond. I figured that he was second-guessing his decision to get under the chair, because he had trapped himself; he could see that I was between him and the door.

Truthfully, at this point, I didn't know what I was going to do or say. The good news was that up to this point, my silent strategy was working. Neither of us knew what to do, and that must have made him even more nervous; he quickly put his head down and tucked it under for safety. That, to me, was an indication that he was pretty smart. I would want to hide from me, too! To rationalize my cluelessness, I decided that I was being silent because I was attempting to do the opposite of what he expected, and it was working, up to a point. The office staff was pleased because he had been wailing two feet from their desks, making it difficult to answer the phones and making parents who were entering the office a little uneasy about dropping their children off at school.

Now, I'm an adult, so I knew we couldn't just stay on the floor and relax all day, so I made the first move. In a very soft, peaceful voice, as though I were waking him up from a deep sleep, I said, "Timothy"—and then waited about twenty seconds. Again, slowly and softly, I said, "Timothy"—and waited.

Quietly and just as slowly as I had spoken, he mumbled, "What?"

I decided to turn the tables a little and be the needy one. Quietly, I kind of whined, "I'm not that comfortable down here on the floor. I was hoping you might get back up on the chair."

No response. I continued: "I'm Mrs. Gatlin, and I look forward to meeting our new fifth graders. I was thinking that you are probably going to be my first student to chat with this year. Trouble is that I chat much better when I am not on the floor. I can tell that you are really upset this morning. How about if we at least just both sit in chairs, and then if you want to chat, we can?"

To my surprise, Timothy obliged and followed me to my office, where he read his book. Later, we talked about his schedule and I showed him around the school. He went to third block and was able to finish the day on his team. I didn't mention anything about the morning's behavior. I decided that morning that my work with Timothy would be to help him be able to end the school year with a different kind of story about himself. By stepping into his world-view, a tenet of the solution-focused approach, I was able to find a way to cooperate with Timothy's needs.

During the first six weeks of school, there were many subsequent episodes with similar characteristics, although each time, Timothy was able to pull himself together much more quickly. We would chat briefly about what had happened; I would ask him to find something he could do differently that would help him get off to a good start in class; and then he would tell me about his books. Then off to class he would go!

By the beginning of the second six weeks, the episodes seemed to be occurring in only one class—the last class of the day. I learned to listen for the buzzer and the voice on the office speaker, asking me to look for Timothy, who had left class again. Usually, I would find him hiding in the library or meet up with him in the hall where he was returning from the drinking fountain. We would sit on the bench in the hall and talk a few minutes, and then he would do his work in my office for the rest of last block.

After several weeks, the student study team recommended that Timothy start fresh on a new team. After Timothy moved to his new team, his behavior stabilized. The teachers on the team, although frustrated that he often did not complete his work, thought that he was interesting and smart and enjoyed having him on their team. The teachers communicated that to Timothy. Timothy told me that he really liked his team.

Several weeks went by, and as I was finishing up some notes, Kenneth, one of my students, whom I will be telling you more about in the section on Tier II, poked his head around the door frame. "Mrs. Gatlin, are you busy? Can I talk to you?"

"You sure can," I said. "Come on in!"

"Mrs. Gatlin," Kenneth began, "there is a boy on our team—Timothy. Do you know him?"

I told him I did.

He quizzed me again with a different inflection: "You *do* know him?"

I told Kenneth that I knew Timothy and that he was a nice person.

"Well, Mrs. Gatlin," he continued. "I am really worried about him. I have been watching him lately. He keeps his head kind of down and his hair covers over his eyes. I think there is something really wrong, and you really need to talk with him."

I thanked Kenneth for being such a caring friend, and I assured him that I would speak with Timothy very soon.

As Kenneth was leaving, I suddenly had a thought. "Kenneth, do you know Timothy pretty well?"

He said that he didn't, but that he would like to.

I offered to have Timothy come in, and Kenneth was really excited about that.

"I want to help him," Kenneth said.

When Timothy came into the office, I introduced the two boys and I told Timothy that Kenneth wanted to meet him. Kenneth looked at Timothy directly and said, "Timothy, I have noticed that you keep your head down with your hair covering your eyes. I used to do that, too." He repeated that last line for emphasis, and then he said, "But I don't do that anymore. Would you want to be my friend?"

Timothy smiled like he had just won a new puppy. Without hesitation, he said, "Yes."

Kenneth had been referring himself to after-school homework detention for the last few weeks. He asked Timothy whether he was interested in doing that, too, and because he was, I phoned Timothy's mom and got permission for him to attend. Kenneth and Timothy went to the detention teacher's room to enroll him. (I sent a secret e-mail to the teacher to let her know what was happening.) The impact on Timothy was pronounced. Not only was he in a positive learning environment, but now he actually had a friend. He had never had a close friend at school.

Having teacher support, encouragement, and overt recognition that he was a valuable member of his team, as well as a friend who would go out of his way to help him, gave Timothy a boost of confidence, the desire to work on self-discipline, and the strength to roll with occasional disappointments. The challenges of intermediate school were greater than Timothy had experienced in fourth grade, but with positive support and the knowledge that people saw his strengths and recognized his competencies, Timothy made huge strides in self-discipline and had only rare setbacks—and they were never of the magnitude of the lapses he had exhibited at the beginning of the year.

Practicing Brief and Effective RTI

Tier I interventions are not always lengthy counseling interventions. Most of the time, they are quick interventions that support the academic goals of the campus. One instance that comes to mind is the homework check. Some students have difficulty getting a homework routine in place at home. Sometimes a quick morning check-in with students is all they need to motivate them to take it seriously. Other times, students may need a check sheet or a reminder sheet to carry in their notebook. Asking students which they prefer works best.

One student I remember had found a workable solution to his problems with homework—he had his parents do it! Noah had his parents convinced that he could not do his homework. He would cry and say it was too hard. His dad would come in to see me, very upset, saying that he and his wife didn't have any home life because they were always doing homework! I knew Noah, and I was familiar with his work and his testing information. I knew that he could handle the work. I was also familiar with the stories about how he wandered around the classroom during independent work time.

With his dad sitting in my office, I sent for Noah. I told him that we had come up with an interesting plan for getting his homework done and that his dad and mom would no longer be helping him.

I told Noah's dad that he and Noah's mom should not pick up a pencil while Noah was doing his math.

Noah's dad questioned me about what would happen if Noah didn't do it.

I replied that Noah would be an even taller fifth-grade student the next year.

Dad clarified that he wasn't supposed to help Noah.

I told him that he had it right. Noah had the ability, and I wanted him to show both his parents and me.

Noah was asked to meet with me the first thing every morning so that I could check on his success. I would check his grades on the computer to make sure that everything was being turned in.

When I saw his father a few weeks later and asked how things were going, he said they were going great. He was beaming with pride that his son actually was able to do the work.

Noah discovered not only that he could do the work and do it well but also that it felt really good to have his dad making such positive comments about him.

In this case, we had to create the context for the exception to be discovered before we had one because the family only had one story to relate to in regard to Noah. I knew that Noah was capable, but his confidence about doing his homework had been sabotaged by his parents' belief that he needed them to help. The parents had always spent their evenings poring over Noah's homework. Because he was now in fifth grade, the homework was beginning to take longer and longer to do. His parents had been describing Noah as "slow in math" and "ADHD" and "little attention span" and "easily frustrated" and even "could be bipolar." They had completely overlooked "capable."

Using Fluid Boundaries to Help Students

Sometimes the lines between Tier I, Tier II, and Tier III seem blurred when it comes to counseling interventions, because some situations are more ongoing than others. Timothy's situation is actually a Tier I intervention, because the counseling that I did with Timothy was a response to reactive behavior. It would be difficult to involve Timothy in a Tier II small-group intervention because he would need some group skills in order to participate and Timothy's challenges in social skills would make a group setting very stressful for him. Now that Timothy has learned to maintain composure and work through some of the challenges of the classroom social scene, a good next step within the general education setting would be to give him some specific social tools to use when working in small groups in class. That would prepare him for being able to function in a Tier II intensive small group to develop social skills.

Tier II Counseling Interventions in RTI

Group Counseling

During the intermediate school years, friendship is the hot topic and girl cliques can be an upsetting source of confusion and drama that can be very disruptive in a class and in a neighborhood. Intermediate school girls are just beginning to form alliances that lock some girls out, and the result is hurt feelings. Study groups and work groups are prevalent at the intermediate level, and in these situations, the girls who are orchestrating cliques can be very sneaky about how they ostracize or criticize a particular girl, who usually is a girl who does not have a reliable friend who will come to her defense. Criticisms usually begin with "No offense, but...." The arguments usually come to a head during physical education. A coach will phone me, saying, "A couple of your frequent flyers need to come and speak with you. They are crying."

When a group can be classified as the frequent flyers' group, that is a good indication that a teachable moment has arrived and it is time to implement a solution-focused Tier II intervention. A Tier II counseling intervention has a systematic plan and purpose. There is an expectation about group leadership, that students listen respectfully and participate in discussion, and the results of the group intervention are evaluated for effectiveness.

The miracle question is a great solution-focused technique to use with Tier II small groups, because it focuses discussion on the outcomes and it gets students working together to come up with ways to make group work more fun and worthwhile. The important thing to remember in implementing a counseling small group is to make sure that the students are doing the thinking and the problem solving, for that is what makes the process solution-focused rather than problem-focused.

Intermediate school students tend to want to turn a group session into a question-and-answer session with the counselor. If the students succeed in doing that, the counselor can expect to see individual students coming into the office, passes in hand, to report, "So-and-so is not doing what you said, and she is ruining our group." The power of a group session comes from the discussion, the group goals, the exploration of the miracle question, and the group search for solutions.

One of the biggest challenges in a small-group intervention is confidentiality. Girls are sometimes tempted to get on the phone and tell everybody what was said in the group. When this happens, the group becomes fragmented. It is important to remind students that confidentiality is paramount to the success of the group. A good practice is to have students sign an agreement that they will honor the rule of confidentiality. They usually kind of like that part because when they sign the confidentiality paper, they feel that their work in the group is important.

Individual Counseling

A Tier II intervention does not have to be a small-group intervention. Sometimes a student has a self-picture that is so self-defeating that it is difficult for the student to find a way out of the cycle of discouraging experiences. In an individual Tier II intervention, a student has regularly scheduled visits and the counselor has close contact with the child's parents.

One example of a Tier II individual intervention involved a boy named Joshua. Joshua was teased and made fun of every day by his peers. Joshua was receiving outside counseling services for depression. He was brought to my attention during the last month of school. I met with him for a few minutes several times a week and kept in close contact with his mother.

I spoke with a number of sixth-grade boys to see whether I could find one who would come to his defense when the teasing started. I spoke to eight boys before I was able to find one who would give it a try. What was surprising was the consistency of response from the other eight boys. They all said that they didn't have enough social standing on the team to be able to stick up for him. When I asked all the boys who on the team did have enough status, they gave me the ninth name. Initially, when I spoke to the ninth boy, he looked very uneasy. When I told him that his name had been given to me as the person who had the most social status on the team and that several people on the team had said that, he looked shocked. I am unsure what occurred later, but the teasing dramatically dropped toward Joshua.

A Tier II counseling intervention often involves a search-and-rescue effort to put a social support mechanism in place for a student who is experiencing a more serious emotional problem. Again, the Tier II intervention is closely watched and evaluated for effectiveness.

Family Counseling

One of the most effective types of Tier II counseling interventions is family counseling. When the family system works together to support the student and build family resilience, the lines of communication open up and the family is able to get on the same page and work toward a common goal. I first met Kenneth (the same Kenneth who befriended Timothy later in the year) during the summer prior to Kenneth's repeat of his fifth-grade year. Kenneth was repeating fifth grade due to his poor TAKS performance, refusal to do work, and refusal to put effort into his work. It isn't easy to pull off a triple header like that! It takes commitment, determination, self-monitoring, self-control—all of the same attributes that it takes to be a great student.

The first time I met Kenneth, he sat with his head down, hair falling into his face, and he was refusing to talk. He was attending summer school, and he was very angry about it. As I eventually discovered, Kenneth was angry about a lot of things—and for good reason.

Kenneth's mother had passed away from a heart attack when he was in third grade. He and his older sister lived with their grandparents, Kenneth's mother's parents. His early years had had little stability. His new home with the grandparents was extremely organized. Kenneth had begun setting fires when he visited his dad, who later became incarcerated. His grandmother was not sure that she and her husband could manage the situation. Kenneth was stuck in a pattern of failure at school and was out of control at home. A further complication was that the grandparents had had no opportunity to grieve for the loss of their daughter because they had been immediately thrust into the parental role of caring for a teenage granddaughter and a preteen grandson.

The grandmother and two children came to the school to meet with me in a family session once a week, beginning in the summer. Eventually, Kenneth began to open up, and gradually, the family came together and began to work together and consider each other's needs. Kenneth's grades went from failing to honor roll, and his discipline problems disappeared. The teachers viewed Kenneth as a very capable young man whom they enjoyed having on their team.

Kenneth was very aware and very proud of the progress he had made in pulling himself together. That is why Kenneth wanted to befriend Timothy when he noticed Timothy at school; he wanted to encourage him and help him feel better about himself. Sometimes children need to be able to pour out what is on their mind and be heard. They need to feel secure in their family and in their relationships at school, or everything gets very confusing for them. It is exciting that Kenneth understood that and realized that what he had learned could be used to help someone else. The Tier II intervention in Kenneth's case was individual and more intense than just individual counseling because the whole family was counseled. Even though this case occurred in a school setting, the family therapy that was conducted there, using a solution-focused approach, was invaluable.

Tier III Interventions

Tier III interventions are the most intensive interventions, which are implemented when Tier I and Tier II interventions have failed to produce enough results. Sometimes Tier III means a referral to the psychologist assigned to our campus or a referral to our campus interventionist, a First Step Counselor. First Step Counselors are assigned to campuses to provide individual intensive counseling for students who are dealing with serious emotional issues. These counselors are licensed professional counselors. They meet with students individually once each week, and they collaborate with the school counselor in order to coordinate the supports available to students. Tier III students are often referred by the school counselor and the student's team of teachers after careful review of exceptions and attempts to integrate strategies using the exceptions as a guide. However, when medical, visual, or other psychological issues intrude, referral to the interventionist is the most helpful. The intermediate and middle school students often have more flexible schedules that allow them to set up visits with an interventionist. Those in districts where an interventionist is a luxury and not a fact may find that the school counselor needs to set weekly sessions with the student or form groups for students with similar issues. Working closely with the team of teachers and using the Level B forms can allow the school counselor to monitor the student and enlist the help of the student's teachers. After several meetings to discuss how the strategies are working, the school counselor may recommend a full assessment for special education if the student does not improve.

The Role of Reflection in Solution-Focused RTI

When we interventionists, school counselors, and RTI team members use a solution-focused approach to RTI, it benefits us to reflect on significant learning experiences that have occurred at different points in our lives. This type of reflection is important because as children move into young adulthood and, later, adulthood, they acquire new understandings of themselves as they prune away earlier thoughts and feelings and replace them with newly found competencies. We practitioners need to reconnect with those thoughts and feelings in ourselves so that we can better understand what our students are attempting to tell us with *their* words and what they are trying to show us with their actions. Human beings, especially young ones, are constantly moving into a dynamic future—one that is on the move, one that provides us with a picture of the world that is in a constant state of revision. We revise our ideas about how life works based on a combination of physical, emotional, and spiritual experiences and understandings that are assimilated almost unconsciously as we move through our personal history. However, when we intentionally look back on some of the significant times that stand out for us, we gain a sense of who we were, what we felt, what we thought at that time and place, and who we are becoming.

Solution-focused RTI promotes such vision. When we revisit some of our memories of growing up and reconnect with the feelings and perceptions associated with the events of our lives, we anchor ourselves in our own experiences, allowing ourselves to be better listeners, empathizers, and questioners, and our experiences equip us with an intuitive eye so that we can recognize strengths in students that are sometimes obscured by the captivating details and compelling nature of the problems looming at the time. In working with children, we have to be able to momentarily break free of the conventional, aged ways that we have learned to perceive, feel, and react, which are woven from the layers of experiences we have acquired between childhood and now. By revisiting early experiences that are similar in feeling to those of students and by remembering how we expressed those feelings, we stand a better chance of reaching students in more significant ways—ways that move them more capably toward their future.

Reprise

On the last day of school each year, over 1,000 fifth-grade and sixth-grade students exit our intermediate school building, this time carrying fraying backpacks with well-worn zippers, ready to be replaced with fresh ones for the next school year. Their packs hold the last of the year's graded assignments and journals filled with notes, reflections, drawings, and an occasional half sheet of paper barely hanging on the spiral wire because the lower half was yanked free to jot down a phone number for a friend. If we have accomplished what we set out to do at the beginning of the year, their packs, though light and easy to maneuver, will be filled with memories and stories to carry with them into their future more confidently than when they entered nine months prior. During their time in school, they will have learned a lot about how school works, about how families work, and about their strengths, their social status, friendship, and trust. And if we have done our job right, they will have a sense that they are interesting and resilient people who should believe in themselves because we believe in them. They will be solution seekers, moving confidently and competently into their future, bursting with limitless possibilities.

Chapter Perspectives to Consider

If a student arrives at intermediate or middle school with challenges that might have been overlooked in elementary school, the world gets a little more demanding. Add in preadolescent changes in body, social life, and interests with the task of being asked to be more responsible in school and there is a disaster waiting to happen.

Yet the solution-focused approach to RTI gives another opportunity to identify challenges without labeling. Instead, such students should be seen as "making it" in spite of the challenges. A student who struggled yet made it through elementary school could be asked about the tools he used to get through. His parents could be asked about the way they supported him and assisted him to make it through. A thoughtful school counselor and team could examine the coping skills and limited academic skills of the student as the student's individual way of succeeding so far, even if it is less than needs to be achieved.

This chapter examined the many ways that solution-focused RTI can change the lives of students and teachers. Could it be a change of classroom venue, with a different teaching style and teacher personality that can transform a troubled student into a compliant one? Could it be that an approach of seeing the "ninth student" as a person who could help stop bullying rather than a person who instigated it as a means of helping a student feeling tormented? Looking at strengths, doing something different, seeking exceptions . . . they belong in the intermediate and middle school and can open still another door to success.

Patricia Gatlin has a master's degree in school counseling from Dallas Baptist University. She is a fellow in the University of California, Irvine, Thinking/Writing Project. She is certified in Texas as a school counselor, a reading specialist, a master reading teacher, English as a second language teacher, elementary and secondary English, and in mid-management. She is a licensed professional counselor-intern and a licensed marriage and family therapist associate. She has been a counselor at Cross Timbers Intermediate School in Mansfield, Texas, for three years.

Chapter 11

Opening the Door to Possibilities in High School

Cassie Reid

The solution-focused approach to RTI looks very different from a high school perspective than from an elementary school perspective, yet it still opens the door for so many possibilities! When we seek the strengths of our high school students instead of their weaknesses, we allow them to see the strengths in themselves.

There are many reasons to provide high school students with the opportunity to see exceptions within themselves through the solution-focused RTI process. Whether it is used in a one-on-one teacher-student conference or in a meeting with parents, solution-focused RTI allows students to see how far they have come and propels them into their desired future. Writing this chapter, I recalled the numerous times I sat across from students who had been told that they couldn't and wouldn't succeed by their teachers. I particularly recall one student named April. She was told by her parents and by every teacher, principal, and other adult in her life that she would not graduate from high school. As her school counselor, I asked April the miracle question, because it seemed as if she needed one. We discussed her miracle, and a world of possibility opened up for her in our discussion. I was able to understand life as she saw it and, in keeping with her miracle goals, provide her with the necessary guidance not only to graduate from high school but get into the college of her choice. April was not the only student to latch on to the solution-focused process. Many other students found that the solution-focused RTI process allowed them to find possibilities with very little searching. It was the educators who needed to take the time to recognize those possibilities within each student.

The Possibility Door Can Be Heavy

When the process of solution-focused RTI was introduced in our district, about the only thing you could hear were moans and groans from all of the faculty and staff. They saw the RTI process as more paperwork, not more possibilities. It took a lot of time, education, and convincing to help the faculty press through the "more work" mind-set and into the "this could make my life so much easier" reality. Many educators are already doing what solution-focused RTI has set out to accomplish and are already successful at implementing powerful strategies and solutions. In working with our high school faculty, it sometimes seemed as if the teachers had adopted the complaining mind-set of students. My office became a dumping ground for students whom they could not handle on their own, at times, especially when the district decided to implement solution-focused RTI for all the students in the district. What I found, however, was that the teachers just didn't understand what they were being asked to do.

I remember one of our science teachers, Pete. He was one of the most disgruntled when he was asked to go to the training for RTI. He explained that he did not understand how the administration could put one more thing on his plate. I used that moment as an opportunity to highlight possibility and his strengths. I talked with him about the things that I noticed when visiting his classroom and speaking with students in his class. I highlighted how he found the good in each student and tailored his teaching to fit each student's needs. In this way, I was able to show him how he was already using the solution-focused RTI model in his daily routine; all he had to do was brag on his skill as a solution-focused RTI educator in his documentation. He continued to come into my office with questions about the RTI model from time to time but never again complained about having to use it. It wasn't because he knew I wouldn't listen; it was because he now had an understanding of what the intervention should look like and was confident that he was already doing it.

So Open a Familiar Door

Solution-focused RTI works with students in the same way that it did with Pete. Many competent, effective teachers create an environment in which their students feel successful, and they don't accept students' complaining and negativity as reality. This attitude allows students to learn how to look for the exceptions and gives them the opportunity to step into their desired reality. These strategies are in keeping with what Tier I is all about.

The solution-focused approach goes hand in hand with many of the core assumptions of traditional RTI at the high school level. For example, RTI posits that high school teachers are students' guide to the future. We provide resources to create an environment in which students can be successful. Another core assumption of RTI is that long-term problems can be prevented with early intervention. Many individuals want to use RTI to address academic issues, but there are many behavioral benefits to this early intervention approach as well, particularly among high school students. Academics are the main concern in a high school, but if a high school student's personal life is not on track, her academic life suffers. I think of the numerous times I spoke with students about a variety of addictions and habits. Amy was one of those students. She loved to come to my office and spent a lot of time there after the death of her father at the beginning of the school year. I enjoyed chatting with Amy, and she always taught me something about what was cool or in style.

I noticed that Amy's visits eventually became less frequent, and I began to hear from others that she was letting a lot of things slide. She had been very invested in softball and was good enough to play in college, yet she had started to lose interest. I decided to speak with her. I talked with her about the strengths I had seen in her. I asked her a rating question about where she saw herself currently, and she said she was at a "4." I asked her where she had seen herself about two months ago, and she said that at that time she had been an "8." I didn't have to say anything else to Amy. She started talking to me about her alcohol abuse. She had used it as a way to cope with the death of her father. She said that no one had even noticed, let alone bothered to ask what was happening with her. We talked about the things she was doing besides alcohol to cope with her pain. We made a list of those things, and Amy agreed to do more of them and less of the alcohol. In a month, she was back to softball and back to being the girl that most people had known at the beginning of the school year. She now plays Division I softball in college.

Amy's case is just one small example of how an early intervention (Tier I) helped keep things from getting out of control. If I had not asked about her and what she was doing to cope with her father's death, she might have continued to allow alcohol to take over the life that she desired. By asking her a rating question and using the RTI principle of early intervention, I was able to help her see that she could cope and change the course of her reality.

Integrating solution-focused concepts and RTI in high school education is something that great school counselors and teachers are doing already. Adopting solution-focused RTI simply means painting the picture so that they are able to see that it isn't more work but simply doing more of what they already do. When introducing RTI to a high school faculty, it is helpful to say, "Many of you are already doing the things that I am about to present. Because you are familiar with the concept of seeking strengths in our students, putting the RTI process in place here will be a snap."

Everyone Is Reachable and Teachable

Another assumption of RTI is that all students can be taught. Unfortunately, as a high school counselor, I had heard many teachers talk about how they had given up on a student because of their academic failings, behavioral problems, or other issues. My biggest challenge was to help teachers see their students as competent, not empty. No student does poorly all of the time; there are some times (exceptions) when unproductive behaviors, academic problems, or other issues are not happening. The solution-focused approach to RTI forces us to see those times and highlight them.

One of my most glowing moments as a school counselor was working with a student named Jay. He was the student whom every teacher came into my office saying they couldn't stand and who they felt would never succeed. They always were speaking negatively about his behavior and academic performance. I allowed them to talk but asked them to try something. I asked them to try just noticing what Jay did well for the next week. I knew Jay from numerous visits in my office and knew he was a great person who just needed to be recognized for that greatness. Jay visited me frequently, and we talked at length about his struggles. I even remember getting reprimanded for the frequency of Jay's visits to my office, but I knew he needed someone to just let him be himself and see his strengths in that process.

Jay and I continued to talk throughout the school year, and Jay continued to be talked about by various personnel in the school. There were a few times when I stuck my neck out for Jay and encouraged the administration and staff just to be patient and look for the strengths in Jay. Some of them would come to my office when they noticed strength in him and share it with me. I was thrilled. I encouraged them to continue seeing the strengths and maybe even tell Jay what they were noticing. Graduation came, and Jay crossed the stage to many cheers from the faculty and staff, some for positive reasons and others out of relief. A few months after graduation, I received a note from Jay. He told me how much the visits to my office had meant to him. He had enrolled in college and had a B average after the first semester. He told me how much hearing about his worth, value, and strengths had meant to him. He said that my office sometimes was the only place where he felt like he had the strengths to do what he wanted to accomplish. He thanked me again. I realized that listening to all of the negativity and encouraging teachers to see Jay's strengths had paid off. He had realized his strengths and noticed how successful he could be.

Jay was the student whom everyone wanted to give up on, and now he has finished a year of college, has a steady job, and is planning on starting his own business in the next couple of years. Solution-focused RTI is all about taking the time to stop and notice students' successes and see students for who they can be, even when they cannot see it.

A Different Kind of Data

RTI assumes that data is what helps us make decisions about students. The data suggested that Jay's future was headed in a negative direction. By encouraging teachers to see exceptions and notice his strengths, I helped them allow a new kind of data to push Jay in a different direction. This is an important piece of being solution-focused in RTI. It is essential to ask yourself, *In what direction do I want the data to push this student?* If we think about it, most of us would choose to push the student to the successful side of the spectrum. Still, too many educators are looking for the negative data, not the positive. They are looking for a way to show the unsuccessful behaviors in order to have that student moved or taken from their responsibility. Educators sometimes look for that negative data to support their hypothesis. But what if educators took it in the opposite direction?

What if educators began to look for the reasons to keep an unsuccessful student in their classroom? Encouraging the teachers to search for the strengths in Jay made their classroom experience with him a much better one. It changed their approach to him and allowed them to see the assets that Jay had to bring to the table. Instead of looking for data to support how unsuccessful Jay was, they began to see the strengths Jay possessed.

Underdogs Get the Bone

I am a bleeding heart when it comes to the underdog student. When RTI arrived on the scene at our high school, many teachers were excited about using it as a tool to get students out of their classroom and prove that these students needed attention and modifications that they could not provide. Yes, it is a difficult job to accommodate each student, but changing the mind-set of the program and teaching the teachers how to use the data differently—to use it *for* the students—is powerful because it benefits both teachers and students. The Level B conversation described in this book allows teachers to talk with a student in a unique way. And students are mesmerized when they are invited to a meeting that is all about them—in a supportive way.

Presentation of solution-focused RTI to a high school faculty is the key. If it is introduced as a way to start thinking about how the tools can be used to make classrooms and schools better than they already are, we will open the door to RTI and its benefits. When introducing the solution-focused approach to teachers, it is essential to highlight what they are already doing well, to affirm that they are already being successful with the difficult students and thus help them understand that RTI is a tool that can only benefit them.

High school counselors have many responsibilities and duties, but being involved in the RTI process is critical for many reasons. In my typical day, for example, I deal with parents who want to meet about their adolescent and tell me all about what their child is not doing. Imagine how different my day might be if teachers started noticing what students were doing well—even if it is only slightly well—and communicated that information to the student's parents. This change in focus would change the whole atmosphere of the school and the frequency of parent concern. If RTI paperwork required teachers to see when the problem isn't happening, they would be less likely to call parents to report negative behavior, because they would not be focused on that anymore! Less reporting of negative behavior would decrease the frequency of meetings with parents, teachers, and students who are concerned about problems and increase meetings in which parents and teachers are bragging about students' successes.

Where Is the Key? Tier I

RTI makes a basic assumption that data drives all decisions made on behalf of the student. Tier I is the data-collecting phase. I found that when working with the teachers, this was the most difficult stage for them to understand. They felt that the students would never be moved to Tier II or qualify for special education services, and until then, they felt lost in regard to how to help students. This perceived gap in the teachers' tool kit of strategies created a great opportunity to present an exception-finding mission. I routinely asked the teachers and other staff members when a student was *not* engaging in the undesired behavior. I wanted them to highlight the times when that student was successful as opposed to pointing out the times when the student was failing or not doing what they wanted the student to be doing. This was a way to introduce solution-focused RTI without them realizing that they were applying a model.

As a former special education teacher, I understand that there are circumstances and situations that require educators to look for behaviors and provide the necessary modifications and classroom setting for that specific individual. I also find that many educators are quick to judge and label students rather than tailor their teaching methods and mental approach to that student in order to find success and strength. In order to do what is best for the student, it is important in Tier I that we not jump to conclusions too soon. RTI is a great process for assessing the needs of our students; we just have to use it in the right way—not as a labeler but as an identifying process.

At the high school level, I find that it is a challenge for educators to avoid labeling students. I remember Mary, a wonderful student who was very bright, sweet, and driven. She would frequent my office and discuss her desire to go to hairdressing school. Many of Mary's teachers would speak with me about her poor academics, poor behavior, and failures. I had a hard time seeing this side of Mary because this Mary did not seem like the same girl who would get all fired up to discuss her goals and aspirations with me; she seemed so driven to succeed when she was in my office. The teachers kept trying to get her mom to agree to special education testing, and they wanted to skip the RTI process altogether. One day, I decided to ask Mary why she thought her teachers talked to me about her grades, behavior, and effort. She laughed out loud and told me it was because they didn't give her a chance to talk. They just assumed that she couldn't do the work, that she didn't want to be in the classroom, and that she wasn't making plans for the future. I asked her why she hadn't shared her hairdressing school dreams with them, and she plainly replied, "What's the point? They only think I am a failure, and they only want to put me in a special education class anyway."

My jaw hit the floor, thinking of the power of the teacher's perceptions to influence Mary's behavior. I decided that some data collection under Tier I would be a great opportunity for Mary and her teachers. I asked each of Mary's teachers to record all of the times when she was working, behaving, and engaging in the classroom. Within one week, the teachers came by my office and started to share Mary's dreams to go to hairdressing school. They were shocked that the girl they had seen in such a negative light was able to dream beyond high school. They saw that Mary actually couldn't wait to graduate. Mary came to my office, beaming. She couldn't believe the difference in the attitudes of her teachers. She accused me of doing something, so I told her that I had only asked them to see what she was doing well. I explained to her how important I thought it was that they see her the way I did.

Not long ago, I heard from Mary. She is enrolled in hairdressing school and loves every minute of it. Thanks to the open minds of her teachers, she was able to avoid a label that she would have carried with her for the rest of her life. She was able to be seen in a different light by her teachers. She was no longer a special education student who had slipped through the cracks all those years but a girl who had dreams, hopes, and ambitions and just needed a few people to believe in her.

Writing about Mary reminds me again of how much power we have as educators. RTI looks slightly different at the high school level because there are more teachers and thus more opportunities to view students' competencies. By the time students get to high school, those needing special education services will have been identified. In high school, therefore, it is assumed that students can succeed in the general education classroom. But that doesn't mean that we should stop there in finding ways to reach them. It is in our hands to provide the tools of success to each of our students. If Tier I is executed as a way for educators to show what students are doing well, it also shows that as educators we truly do have the best interests of students in mind, that we are being student-focused instead of problem-focused.

Using solution-focused RTI in Tier I is the perfect way to introduce a whole different atmosphere to your high school. It is a way to change the mind-set of the teachers, staff, and administration so that they begin to see the RTI process as a way to look for the strengths and successes of the students they encounter each day. It becomes a data-seeking mission, not to find the behaviors that we want to change but to find the behaviors that we want to happen more frequently. It is truly a way to revolutionize the school setting with a mandated program. RTI is something that will exist no matter what our opinion. Why not make it a process that allows our students to grow and step into a brighter future?

Think about the Tier I materials you have seen for your school. Look at the materials and what the focus tends to be in most of the paperwork. Typically, the paperwork focuses on problems. If we shift the paperwork to record how frequently the student is doing a desired task or behavior, think about how differently we would approach the data collection process. I feel that this information-gathering process is where our active listening skills and true distinguishing skills come into play. It is important to understand when a problem is a problem, but regardless of the situation, there are still strengths that each student demonstrates on a daily basis. Solution-focused RTI aims to find those strengths and reinforce them.

Sometimes Opportunity's Door Has a Couple of Locks: Tier II

RTI also adheres to the principle that data must drive the movement of a student from Tier I to Tier II. In Tier II, a meeting with parents, teachers, and the student occurs. The student's input is one of the most valuable resources that we can use. Students know best what they need, and they often just need a context in which to share their ideas. Solution-focused Level B meetings provide a chance to collaborate differently with parents, students, teachers, and staff. As the school counselor, I led the solution-focused RTI meetings so that I could mediate and set the tone for the discussion. When the tone of the meeting is set as solution-focused rather than problem-focused, everyone in attendance benefits. In order to stay aligned with the students and ease their anxiety, I typically met with them individually on the day before or the day of the meeting. I told them what the meeting would be about and asked them to think of what they wanted everyone to know about what they needed. This way, the student understood that no matter what was said by others in the meeting, I was an ally and was in their corner.

One part of the solution-focused RTI meeting that I enjoyed was asking exception questions. The parents were always shocked when I asked them about times when their child was doing well. They were programmed to talk about problems in school meetings and rarely were asked to praise their child. The teachers were used to my asking about times when the poor behavior was not occurring, so they weren't as shocked as the parents.

I particularly remember one meeting that we had for Joe. He was a great student, and the teachers had done an exceptional job in highlighting his strengths and documenting times when he was successful in the classroom. He knew that they had been looking for his good behavior and excellent academic skills, and he showed them. He was more worried about his parents. I opened the meeting by asking the teachers and his parents about things they noticed in Joe that they appreciated. Joe's reaction was priceless. He started the meeting slumped in his chair, shoulders down. But from the time that I asked the question about exceptions until the end of the meeting, when we talked more about his strengths, he sat up and felt very at ease in being a part of the meeting. He left the meeting that some had thought would focus on his problem feeling better than he had when he came in. This meeting for Joe is a prime example of how a Level B meeting in Tier II of RTI should go.

In keeping with Tier II, the meeting for Joe also focused on what he needed to be more successful in the classroom. This transition from what he was doing well to what he needed to do more often in order to improve came about through the miracle question. This is another great question to ask because it gives the student, family, and teachers a whole new perspective. It is important to see how changes in behavior and academics on a miracle day would affect the system represented by those in the meeting. What would it look like if the student were able to complete all of his work? How would that be helpful to the teachers, parents, and student? What would be different for the student? By asking the miracle question, the attendees of the Level B meeting are able to see how these behavioral changes would positively affect the atmosphere and future of the system. Thinking in this way keeps the family, school personnel, and student all in a future-focused state of mind. It allows them to think about the time when the problems will no longer be a part of their lives. This vision allows them to remain open to possibilities and helps them adopt the mind-set that the problem is extinguishable.

Stop, Think, and Dream About a Miracle

Just for a moment, stop and think about your toughest student. Some tough students take a lot of TLC to crack. Think about that student, and think about how a meeting all about how he or she could get exactly what they want would be beneficial. No matter what kinds of students we encounter in a high school, all of them are open and ready to discuss what they want and how they want to get there. Their strategies are not always in sync with ours, and therein lies some confusion and frustration. The miracle question helps us to step out of confusion and frustration for just enough time to dream of a better day. Think about the behavior interventions and other meetings you have attended in regard to student performance. They probably were are all problem-focused, and typically, you left feeling defeated, hoping that the suggested interventions would work. Imagine how a student feels when they are part of a meeting like that. They can't please anyone, and no matter what they do, they will always be unsuccessful. This negative cycle is why it is so important that we change the mind-set and atmosphere in the meetings that move a student from Tier I to Tier II. When we allow a student to paint a picture of what they want by answering the miracle question, we put them in control of their future and in control of their miracle.

Once you have asked the student, parent, and school personnel how the miracle would be helpful to them, listen for the answers, for they will become actions and strategies. The student can conceptualize what he will be doing in order to achieve the miracle on a small scale. A rating question can be used here as well. When I asked Joe what his miracle would look like, he was able to state specific details of what it would involve. I then asked him to rate on a scale of 1 to 10 where he was in relation to the miracle: "1" meant that he hadn't even started working toward the miracle, and "10" meant that the miracle was a reality. He said he was at "5," and surprisingly, his teachers agreed. They then chimed in as to what he had been doing to move from the bottom to a "5." It was great for Joe to see that they had been noticing his successes and documenting all he had done to improve. I then asked Joe what he would need to do to get from a "5" to a "6." He started naming different things that he could do, like getting some tutoring, checking his behavior, completing homework. His list was exactly what we needed from the meeting. He was able to conceptualize his actions and what he would be doing as opposed to being told by the group what they wanted for him. We spent some more time finalizing Joe's plan for achieving the miracle. He came up with the idea of attending one-on-one tutoring sessions on his own. Do you think he went? Absolutely, because he had come up with the idea and there was value in it for him. He was able to see that by going to the tutoring and doing what was asked of him, he would have the outcome he desired. It was rewarding for everyone in the meeting, because the focus was on the solution and not on the problem.

In Tier II, I find it essential to keep in contact with the parents of my students. Their input about what is happening at home can only help to bring about the miracle the student desires. It is also good to maintain contact with the parents in order to help them stay solution-focused as opposed to problem-focused. Constantly reminding parents to look for times when their child is successful keeps the miracle in sight. I follow up with my students in the RTI process often, in order to keep the miracle fresh in their mind. These reminders of their vision helps to keep them from being discouraged and distracted.

At times, we will encounter a student who requires the services that Tier III provides. It is imperative to remain solution-focused when an individual requires more services. We still want to look for what that student does well in order to keep her in the least restrictive environment. Many educators feel that once a student requires Tier III services, she is well on her way to being removed from the classroom setting, but this does not have to be the case. This is truly the time for the counselor and other school personnel to become even more involved with the student's situation in order to create an environment for change.

Tier III is simply a form of differentiated instruction that provides a student with opportunities to demonstrate his strengths and successes. It allows a student to receive individualized attention and modifications in order to get him back to the mainstream classroom. This has been the goal all along, to place students in the least restrictive environment, allowing them to learn with their peers. In our school, very few students needed to go past Tier II.

Keeping the Door Open to Opportunity

I have worked with many students, and the power of individual attention is underrated. Many students have come to my office and talked about the quality time they have spent in tutorials with their teacher, which gave them the individual time they craved. Individual sessions allowed students to feel supported and understood and gave them an opportunity to be successful. Students told me how much easier the information would become once it was explained to them individually as opposed to the entire class. Individual attention is one reason why Tier I and Tier II interventions work so well in a high school setting. Once students identify what they need and the teachers begin accommodating them, the students improve.

Merging the solution-focused approach and RTI forms a powerful tool for high schools. The difference in the school environment can be experienced by every member of the faculty, staff, and administration when the solution-focused mind-set takes over. The future can be changed for so many students when we are willing to take just a few extra minutes to see the strengths and positive behaviors they demonstrate daily. If we are willing to collect data in this fashion, we can only help our students become more successful and provide them with an atmosphere for change. RTI may not have initially been presented as a powerful key, but it can certainly become the key that opens the door to the desired future of our students, staff, and parents.

Chapter Perspectives to Consider

If you were to gather elementary, middle, and high school teachers into one room and talk to them about interventions that lead to success, chances are that the elementary school teachers would be more likely to ask what the students need. The secondary school teachers would be more likely to talk about what the students need to do. This difference in placing responsibility on the student, or sitting back and waiting for success or failure without asking students what they need from their teacher can make the difference in a successful high school career for a challenged student.

Solution-focused RTI in the high school does look different than in the elementary school, as those students in high school are often mistaken for being unmotivated or lazy, rather than needing additional help. Yet imagine the impact on a high school student when his teacher asks him what he needs. Most adolescents who struggle in high school are used to being told what they need to do or else they won't graduate. But imagine a thoughtful counselor who takes the time to sit and ponder exceptions and then find ways to converse with teachers about those exceptions. The high school student who developmentally is about how he is perceived by others suddenly feels perceived as having a chance and that is very motivating! Be that teacher or school counselor who takes the time to inquire about a student's abilities outside of school, at home, with friends, and in hobbies or extracurricular activities. The outcome may turn out to be exceptional for both you and your student.

Cassie Reid, M.Ed., LPC-I, is a certified school counselor who has worked with elementary and high school students in the Keller Independent School District in Keller, Texas. Prior to becoming a school counselor, Cassie was a behavior modifications teacher who worked with special education students. She is finishing her Ph.D. in family therapy at Texas Woman's University and is a clinician in the University of Texas system. She consults with private schools, helping them to establish solution-focused counseling and education programs, and she is a therapist for a camp where she helps elementary-age children through the grief process.

Chapter 12

Getting Buy-In

As described throughout this book, when the climate of a school is focused on visions of the future, seeing past problems to when school works, faculty members become more productive and more hopeful and experience a renewed sense of caring for their students. Yet, how can just one person enlist a faculty to become solution focused? The solution-focused approach touts that there is a ripple effect when one person begins to change her outlook, behaviors, and approach to relating to others. Let's examine next what an alternative high school did to implement the ideas of the solution-focused approach with its faculty and its students, creating an environment that not only won national awards in the process, but graduated successful students.

Risk New Ways of Relating for Better Results

At Gonzalo Garza Independence High School in Austin, Texas, a solution-focused alternative school for at-risk students, the mission statement says it all: "Gonzalo Garza Independence High School shall foster a community of empowered learners in an atmosphere of mutual respect and trust where each individual is challenged to learn, grow, and be successful now and in the future" (Austin Independent School District, n.d.).

Students are given a code of honor when they enroll. Teachers respect their students and do not boss them. Instead, they lead them by respecting them and going above and beyond to assist them. The solution-focused approach is the underlying foundation. As a result, only one fight has occurred in the last ten years at Garza. Students pass their achievement tests. A high percentage of students at Garza go on to college (Austin Independent School District, n.d.).

What happens at Garza can happen at any school that uses the solution-focused approach. However, it requires a new mind-set. Instead of trying to fit each student into a certain box so that they can be taught like other students, it takes asking the students to describe the kind of box that they need. This kind of dialogue is a new process for educators, for it puts teachers and administrators in the role of non-experts and positions students and parents as the experts.

While that shift is scary at first, it leads to new ways of relating and more success than ever before. To promote such an environment, the faculty must be engaged in learning how the process works, and nothing works better than letting them experience it personally. To accomplish this, it is vital that they are involved from the beginning, processing what their school will look like in the future when students learn and teachers are able to teach.

Start at the Top

Whether your role is that of a school counselor, special education coordinator, administrator, or teacher, if implementing a solution-focused approach to RTI is what you wish to pursue, talk to the boss first. Most principals are open to hearing new ideas that will improve their school's performance. Across the country, many schools are dealing with high percentages of students being placed into special education. When schools have an accelerated number of students placed in special education, often the state board of education raises an eyebrow and conjures up an investigation. No district wants that to happen.

Therefore, as you begin a conversation with the principal, mention that RTI is not going away and is in fact soon to be mandated across the country. Mention that you have noticed an abundance of paperwork and some disillusioned teachers who have not found the current RTI process helps students. Ask the principal if you could leave this book with him for review. Set an appointment the following week for another conference with the principal.

Then, come back a week later to ask about the principal's thoughts. Hope by then that the principal has had a chance to look over the book and you can propose pitching the idea of solution-focused RTI to the faculty at the next faculty meeting. Ask for the principal's support at the meeting. Get yourself on the schedule at the next meeting.

From this point, do your homework by considering people in your school building who you know are people with influence. Talk to them individually and let them know that you need their support in implementing the approach. Tell them that the next faculty meeting will be an important one and that if they like what you say to show their interest and desire to try out the process.

Then, gather your thoughts, bring your confidence, and set out to produce a ripple effect.

Start with a Miracle by Asking for One

The miracle question (de Shazer, 1985) is a goal-setting question often used by solution-focused therapists. The strength of the question lies in its ability to take the client into another world momentarily, imagining how life would be different without the problem. This sense of freedom allows the client to brainstorm and describe to the therapist whatever his heart desires.

The same opportunity evolves when a faculty member is asked the miracle question. The staff is asked the question in an attempt to get them to envision a school where they can become the teachers they want to be. When I am asked by school administrators how to boost morale in their school or how to get the faculty on board with a new program, I usually say to the administrator, "What would your faculty say it would take?" Too often, we assume that we know which strategies and interventions will produce a certain result and forget to ask the staff we serve to provide us with the answer. Then, when our ideas don't work, we blame the staff.

The miracle question is merely one part of the solution-focused process that this book embraces for the purpose of creating an RTI program that fits the students in your school. Asking the miracle question as you begin to develop a solution-focused RTI program for your school will yield countless answers. Consider asking your staff a question like this: "Suppose we all go home tonight and relax. While we sleep, a miracle occurs. When we return to school tomorrow, we all find that our RTI program is working well for our students and for ourselves. What do each of you think would be happening that would tell us that this was the case?"

You might get answers like this:

There would be less paperwork.

Students would be cooperative.

Parents would be attending the RTI meetings.

We would feel support in the interventions.

Our referrals to special education would be lower.

Students who really needed special education would be tested.

Let's look at the first answer, "There would be less paperwork." Many teachers will explain that the paperwork involved in RTI is enormous. There are assessments, interventions, more assessments, and more interventions, and the interventions are typically developed by teachers alone. But what if the paperwork was substantially less? Most teachers would probably say that they would be more inclined to do it. In solution-focused RTI, the paperwork is very limited because there is less focus on problem talk and more on solution talk, quickly setting goals and identifying exceptions.

The second answer, "Students would be more cooperative," reveals a need for teachers to feel that they are collaborating with students. In solution-focused RTI, collaboration between student and teacher is the core process. As teachers and students begin having solution-focused conversations that focus on what the student needs rather than what the teacher needs (or what the teacher says the student needs), relationships change. A teacher who looks for competencies (exceptions to the problem) in a student often finds much more collaboration and cooperation after telling the student her complimentary observations. Teachers also collaborate by conferring with colleagues about their discoveries on what works for students.

Now take the following opening exercise and use it in your first conversation with your faculty to initiate such a climate in your school.

More Exercises to Create Buy-In

The next few pages contain more exercises that describe the solution-focused RTI process and help faculty members understand the process. Use the exercises during follow-up faculty meetings to continue providing information on the solution-focused process and keep interest going.

The fun "eBay Exercise" is a great exercise to use to help teachers begin to see their students differently. This will be very helpful as you begin the Level A, B, and C meetings that focus primarily on identifying exceptions. Seeking exceptions takes a new lens and seeing past problem-focused times.

Proceed to Level A, B, and C

After the initial exercises are completed, pass out a copy of "Solution-Focused RTI at a Glance," provided in Appendix A, and explain the process and how it is based on the original concept of RTI.

Stay Focused on Implementation

It will be important for you to sit in on Level A conferences whenever possible to assist your faculty members in staying solution focused. Also sit in on Level B meetings to make sure that each member present stays focused on the goal and exceptions. Should someone venture into problem talk, try saying: "Thank you for your observations. While your comment is very important, it is also important to talk about when the problem isn't occurring as often. Can we do that now? Who would like to start?"

You are taking your faculty to a new level by helping them become solution focused in the RTI process. Some of them will grasp the ideas quickly and others may struggle. Stay patient and compliment them for their diligence and attempt to complete the process.

Buy-In Exercise: The Miracle School

1. Read the following question to your faculty:

   Suppose we all go home tonight and relax. While we sleep, a miracle occurs. When we return to school tomorrow, we all find that our RTI program is working well for our students and for ourselves. What do each of you think would be happening that would tell us that this was the case?

2. Write down ALL of the answers on a whiteboard so everyone can see their contributions.

   _____

   _____

   _____

   _____

   _____

3. Ask the faculty, How will these miracles make a difference to them? Write down the answers.

   _____

   _____

   _____

   _____

4. Thank the faculty for their time. Mention that you will begin implementing a new approach to RTI during the next few weeks. Tell them that they will get more instruction soon. Tell them that they will not be expected to learn it on their own and you will be there every step of the way to help. Tell them the process will include their ideas, which you hope will make their days and involvement in RTI less stressful.

The eBay Exercise

Say: "In pairs, discuss a student whom you remember as being particularly difficult this year. We can call him or her the *nightmare student.* Take turns writing down the problems you had with the student."

Say: "With problems like these, how would you work with that student if he or she showed up at your classroom door this fall?"

Say: "Now, together, write an advertisement for the student on eBay, highlighting all of his or her best features."

Say: "If a student with that description shows up at your door this fall, how would you work with him or her?"

Have the faculty work on the exercise for about fifteen minutes. Thank them for their work. Ask them what they learned from the exercise. Hopefully, you will get answers such as "When you don't think too negatively, you get further with a student." Acknowledge that the way we describe students and parents influences how we work and relate with them. Write down the faculty's answers and compliment them profusely on their brilliance.

Pass out copies of "How to Focus Your Conversation on Solutions." Suggest to the faculty that they keep in mind the eBay description and begin to think about how having a conversation of the type outlined on the handout might be helpful in a parent conference.

Ask the group to get back into pairs and try out the process. They are to pretend that one person is the eBay student (or the student's parent) and that the other is the teacher. Allow them about fifteen minutes for the discussion. Once finished, ask the faculty how the conversation they just had was different from most parent conferences. Answers should center on the questions being more positive, respectful, and so on. If they do, point out the similarities and, again, compliment the faculty.

Tell the group that the questions center on something called the *solution-focused approach,* which builds on times when students are slightly successful. Tell them that the approach sees students and parents as experts and that it places more responsibility on students and parents, leaving the teacher in the role of supporter. Ask the faculty whether they would be willing to try the process for a semester, as an experiment. Show them the one-page "Solution-Focused RTI Process at a Glance." Share with them how the process works. Let them know that the Level A, B, and C meetings are very similar to the role playing they just did. Also mention that paperwork is minimal in this process!

How to Focus Your Conversation on Solutions

Step 1: Talk About the Concern

"What can we talk about *right now* that would help you [or your child] to be more successful? I care about what you think and what you need from me."

_____

_____

_____

Step 2: Set a Goal Together

"Tell me what it would look like on a small scale when things get better in the near future."

_____

_____

_____

_____

"What difference will that make?"

_____

_____

_____

_____

Step 3: Identify the Exceptions Together

"Take me back to a time when a little of that happened. What was different then? What did you do differently? What did other people do?"

_____

_____

_____

_____

(continued)

Step 4: Ask the Scaling Question

"On a scale of 1 to 10, with '1' meaning that things are not working and '10' meaning that things are perfect, where are things now in relation to your goal?"

_____

_____

_____

_____

_____

Step 5: Set a Task for a Short Time Period

"On that same scale, where would you like to be in [one day, one week]?"

_____

_____

_____

_____

_____

"What can you do to begin to make that happen?" (Go over the exception list as a reminder, if necessary.)

_____

_____

_____

_____

_____

Source: Adapted from Metcalf, 2008b.

Solution-Focused RTI at a Glance

The following process includes all three RTI tiers.

Step 1: Teacher or parent notices a student not succeeding in a subject (or subjects) as expected for the current grade level. A Level A meeting is held with the primary teacher, student, and parent. The student is rated each week for three weeks on a scale of 1 to 10 in which 10 means completely successful. If the student's rating score increases after three weeks, Level A meetings continue until the teacher sees a level of success that is deemed appropriate.

Step 2: If Level A interventions do not result in better scores on the 10-point scale, a Level B meeting is held, including each of the student's teachers, the student, and the parent. The student is rated each week by each of the teachers. If the rating score increases, Level B meetings continue until the student reaches a level of success deemed appropriate by the team.

Step 3: If Level B interventions do not result in better scores on the 10-point scale, a Level C meeting is held, including each of the student's teachers, the student, the parent, and community resource staff such as education service center consultants, school psychologists, hearing or vision screening staff, or social workers. This more evaluative assessment may also include the development of a solution-focused IEP.

At this point, have "Solution-Focused RTI Conversation: Level A" templates available for distribution, along with "Exception Findings: Level A" forms. Explain the importance of the Exception Findings sheet in the process of identifying exceptions on a daily basis. Explain that it is that sheet that will be helpful in the next level conversations if it is necessary to move up one level.

Designate a place where teachers can come to gather the forms for Level A, Level B, and Level C meetings. The school counselor's office might be a good place because the school counselor typically is involved in Level B and Level C meetings.

Chapter Perspectives to Consider

In every school, there are teachers who are always supportive of trying out new ideas. I refer to these teachers as "the miracle workers." You know who they are. They rarely refer students to the office for discipline because they have such phenomenal classroom management skills and because they build terrific relationships with their students. When implementing the solution-focused RTI program, invest in some time in talking with these miracle workers at your school prior to the faculty meeting at which you introduce the ideas. Ask them for their support. Also ask them, "Based on your knowledge of our faculty, what would you suggest as some ways to ask them to try out a new approach?"

Then, just do it. Follow their advice. You may have noticed throughout this book and in the solution-focused RTI process that there is heavy reliance on asking, "What do you suggest?" That's because the heart and soul of this process is to ask those we need to serve how we can serve them best. Therefore, here are some thoughts to consider for this chapter:

- What initiatives have been well received by faculty in the past?
- Why did those initiatives work well, according to the majority of faculty members?
- What would faculty members say that they need from me in an initiative like solution-focused RTI?
- Who are the miracle workers in my school?

Helping your school to become solution-focused in RTI will provide you and your fellow faculty members, students, and parents new opportunities for not only seeing students differently, but also experiencing more chances for success. Most schools that have implemented this process find that the disciplinary referrals drastically decrease. Faculty members who use the solution-focused process in RTI start using it when conversing with their students and among themselves. The atmosphere changes, the community recognizes the change, and parents become more involved.

Sound like a miracle waiting to happen at your school? It is.

Afterword

This book has been written for classroom teachers, students, and parents in order to simplify the RTI process and add a focus on solutions that empowers everyone involved. My intention is to give every student an opportunity to show their competencies to the educators in their lives who will make decisions with them about their futures. Problem-focused approaches do not always create hope, for they cast spells over children in the form of labels. The solution-focused approach in this book has been proven to raise student and teacher morale in Davenport Community Schools year after year, lowering special education admissions in the process.

There will always be students whose challenges warrant special education services, and they should always receive them! However, if other children who are slightly challenged can function in the general education classroom with just a few additional interventions, why not try? When those students begin to succeed, both student and teacher get the credit. When it comes to building self-esteem and confidence, it doesn't get much better than that.

Appendix A: Reproducible Forms to Help with the RTI Process

This section contains reproducible forms for the solution-focused RTI meetings that have been presented throughout this book. They are arranged in the order that they can be used.

Solution-Focused RTI at a Glance

The basic ideas that follow explain how solution-focused RTI fulfills the expectations of districts that educators will gather data, develop strategies, and review outcomes.

Tier I

Objective: The teacher is to differentiate instruction, and provide instruction designed to meet the specific needs of all students.

Solution-focused RTI: On a scale of 1 to 10, with "10" being the highest, the teacher rates the effectiveness of lesson plans, delivery of instruction, activities, and incentives to succeed through self-reflection and student input on a weekly basis.

The teacher deletes activities that do not work and implements more of the activities that have been identified as ones that work.

Tier II

Objective: The teacher or team Implements instructional programs that are aimed at developing a student's skills through the use of groups or additional coaching.

Solution-focused RTI: The teacher or team finds out how colleagues approach challenged students with even slight success, and implements or integrates those strategies with research-based curriculum to raise the student's skill level. The teacher or team uses the 1–10 scale to rate the student's success in the classroom with the student on a weekly basis. The teacher or team inquires of the student and his or her parent how the student learns best, and searches for times and situations when the student is more successful, inside or outside the classroom.

Tier III

Objective: The teacher or team provides a higher level of instruction and evaluation to students who have not been responsive to Tier II interventions.

Solution-focused RTI: The teacher or team uses solution-focused conversation to continually seek exceptions, inviting the student and his or her parent to participate in team meetings. In addition, the teacher or team invites special education teachers to assist classroom teachers in applying research-based curriculum to exceptions. The teacher or team or diagnostician encourages exploration of health issues such as hearing, vision, or allergies.

Student Survey

Name: _____   Date: _____

Please answer the following questions. You may use additional paper if necessary.

1. What is your favorite subject in school, and why?

_____

_____

2. Would you rather hear a story, read a story, or watch the story acted out, as in a play or movie?

_____

3. What do you enjoy the most about your school day? Explain.

_____

_____

_____

4. What do you do for fun outside of school? (hobbies, activities)

_____

_____

_____

5. Tell me about a personal accomplishment that made you proud.

_____

_____

_____

6. Tell me what else you do well.

_____

_____

_____

7. What can I (as your teacher) do to help you be successful?

_____

_____

_____

8. What will you (as the student) do to help yourself be successful?

_____

_____

_____

Learning Feedback

Name (optional): _____   Date: _____

Please answer the following questions. You may use additional paper if necessary.

Lesson or unit: _____

1. What about this lesson or unit do you remember best?

   _____

2. What did we do in class that really helped you to understand the information?

   _____

   _____

3. What can I as your teacher do more of that would help you continue to be successful?

   _____

   _____

   _____

4. What can you as a student do more of that would help you continue to be successful?

   _____

   _____

   _____

5. On a scale of 1 to 5 (1 = not at all; 5 = very well), how would you rank your understanding of this lesson? Please circle one.

   1 = Did not understand
   2 = Understood some
   3 = Understood half
   4 = Understand almost all
   5 = Understood everything

6. On a scale of 1 to 5 (1 = none; 5 = all), how much effort did you put into learning this lesson? Please circle one.

   1 = none
   2 = some
   3 = half
   4 = almost all
   5 = all

Solution-Focused RTI at a Glance

The following process includes all three RTI tiers.

Step 1: Teacher or parent notices a student not succeeding in a subject (or subjects) as expected for the current grade level. A Level A meeting is held with the primary teacher, student, and parent. The student is rated each week for three weeks on a scale of 1 to 10 in which 10 means completely successful. If the student's rating score increases after three weeks, Level A meetings continue until the teacher sees a level of success that is deemed appropriate.

Step 2: If Level A interventions do not result in better scores on the 10-point scale, a Level B meeting is held, including each of the student's teachers, the student, and the parent. The student is rated each week by each of the teachers. If the rating score increases, Level B meetings continue until the student reaches a level of success deemed appropriate by the team.

Step 3: If Level B interventions do not result in better scores on the 10-point scale, a Level C meeting is held, including each of the student's teachers, the student, the parent, and community resource staff such as education service center consultants, school psychologists, hearing or vision screening staff, or social workers. This more evaluative assessment may also include the development of a solution-focused IEP.

At this point, have "Solution-Focused RTI Conversation: Level A" templates available for distribution, along with "Exception Findings: Level A" forms. Explain the importance of the "Exception Findings" sheet in the process of identifying exceptions on a daily basis. Explain that it is that sheet that will be helpful in the next level conversations if it is necessary to move up one level.

Designate a place where teachers can come to gather the forms for Level A, Level B, and Level C meetings. The school counselor's office might be a good place because the school counselor typically is involved in Level B and Level C meetings.

RTI Documentation: Tier I Intervention

Date: _____

Student: _____   Grade: _____   Homeroom: _____

Date	Areas for Tier I Intervention	Student's Strengths	Interventionist	Minutes per Day	Methods	Solutions Discovered	Assessment 1 = Needs intervention; 2 = Making progress; 3 = Mastered
Week:							
Week:							
Week:							

Recommendations: _____

_____

Student will receive: _____ Regular instruction _____ Tier I Tier II _____ (Circle appropriate level of intervention.)

Student will / will not (circle one) be re-assessed in _____ weeks.

Completed by _____ Date: _____

RTI Documentation: Tier II Intervention

Date: _____

Student: _____

Grade: _____

Homeroom: _____

Date	Areas for Tier II Intervention	Student's Strengths	Interventionist	Minutes per Day	Methods and Programs (Research-Based)	Solutions Discovered	Assessment 1 = Needs intervention; 2 = Making progress; 3 = Mastered
Week:							
Week:							
Week:							

Recommendations: _____

_____

_____

Student will receive: _____ Tier I Tier II _____ (Circle appropriate level of intervention.)

Student will / will not (circle one) be re-assessed in _____ weeks.

Completed by _____ Date: _____

RTI Documentation: Tier III Intervention

Date: _____

Student: _____   Grade: _____   Homeroom: _____

Date	Areas for Tier III Intervention	Student's Strengths	Interventionist	Minutes per Day	Methods and Programs (Research-Based)	Solutions Discovered	Assessment 1 = Needs intervention; 2 = Making progress; 3 = Mastered
Week:							
Week:							
Week:							

Recommendations: _____

_____

_____

Student will receive: _____ Tier I Tier II _____ Referral to _____ (Circle appropriate level of intervention.)

Student will / will not (circle one) be re-assessed in _____ weeks.

Completed by _____   Date: _____

Copyright © 2010 by John Wiley & Sons, Inc.

Solution-Focused RTI Conversation: Level A

Date: _____

Student: _____ Grade: _____

Primary teacher: _____ Team: _____

Attendees (parent, teacher, and student):

_____

_____

1. **Identify hopes:** The teacher opens by expressing appreciation to those attending the meeting, then starts the conversation: *"What are your best hopes for our meeting today?"*

   (It is common for attendees to answer by saying what they do *not* want. Help those who respond in this way to develop a more workable goal by asking, "What do you want to happen instead?")

   Parent: _____

   Student: _____

   Teacher: _____

   "On a scale of 1 to 10, with '1' being not successful and '10' being completely successful, where is the student in regard to what we want to achieve?"

   Parent: _____ Student: _____ Teacher: _____

2. **Set goals:** The teacher thanks the parent and student for their responses and asks, *"What will the student be doing in the classroom over the next three weeks so that the score increases and our concern decreases?"*

   Parent: _____

   _____

   Student: _____

   _____

   Teacher: _____

   _____

3. **Identify exceptions:** The teacher asks about times when behavior or performance as described in the goal occurs or has occurred in school or at home: *"When is this happening or when has it happened slightly already in other classrooms, grades, or situations at school or even outside of school?"*

(continued)

Solution-Focused RTI Conversation: Level A (*Continued*)

Parent: _____

_____

Student: _____

_____

Teacher: _____

_____

4. **Develop strategies:** The teacher, parent, and student then decide which exceptions can be used and adapted in the classroom and at home for the next few weeks.

   Classroom strategies:

   _____

   _____

   Curriculum addition based on exceptions:

   _____

   _____

   Home strategies:

   _____

   _____

5. **Set targets:** The teacher restates the rating scores from the beginning of the conversation and asks the parent and student what scaling they hope the student will achieve by the end of the next week.

   Parent: _____ Student: _____ Teacher: _____

   Summary: The teacher asks the parent and student, *"What was helpful for you today in this conversation?"*

   Parent: _____

   _____

   Student: _____

   _____

   Next meeting date: _____ Time: _____

Source: Adapted from Metcalf, 2008b.

Exception Findings: Level A

Date: _____

Student: _____ Grade: _____

The documentation on this page is *only* for exceptions—times, situations, or activities when the student begins to be more successful in the classroom.

Week 1 Exceptions: List activities, situations, or assignments:

1. _____
2. _____
3. _____
4. _____
5. _____

Weekly score: _____ Student: _____ Teacher: _____

Week 2 Exceptions: List activities, situations, or assignments:

1. _____
2. _____
3. _____
4. _____
5. _____

Weekly score: _____ Student: _____ Teacher: _____

Week 3 Exceptions: List activities, situations, or assignments:

1. _____
2. _____
3. _____
4. _____
5. _____

Weekly score: _____ Student: _____ Teacher: _____

Exception Observations: Level B

Student: _____   Teacher: _____

Dear Teacher,

There will be a solution-focused RTI Level B meeting for _____

_____ on _____

at _____ in room _____. Your presence is requested because you are an important member in the student's academic life. The meeting will not last longer than thirty minutes.

Prior to the meeting, please notice times when this student is slightly successful in your classroom. Note the kinds of lessons, activities, behavioral interventions, motivational strategies, or other methods that help the student be slightly more successful. These "exceptions" to times when the student is less successful should be listed below. Please list at least five exceptions below, and bring the list to the meeting.

Thank you.

_____

Exceptions:

1. _____

_____

2. _____

_____

3. _____

_____

4. _____

_____

5. _____

_____

Solution-Focused RTI Conversation: Level B

Date: _____

Student: _____ Grade: _____

Primary teacher: _____ Team: _____

Attendees:

_____

_____

1. **Identify hopes:** The leader opens by expressing appreciation to those attending the meeting and then starts the conversation: *"What are your best hopes for our meeting today?"*

   (It is common for attendees to answer by saying what they do *not* want. Help those who respond in this way to develop a more workable goal by asking, "What do you want to happen instead?")

   _____

   _____

   _____

   _____

   _____

   _____

   Parent: _____ Student: _____ Teachers (take average score):

   _____ School counselor: _____

2. **Set goals:** The leader thanks everyone for their responses and asks, *"What will the student be doing in the classroom over the next three weeks so that the score increases and our concern decreases?"*

   "On a scale of 1 to 10, with '1' being not successful and '10' being completely successful, where is the student in regard to what we want to achieve?"

   _____

   _____

   _____

(continued)

Solution-Focused RTI Conversation: Level B (*Continued*)

3. **Identify exceptions:** The leader asks about the exceptions that everyone present was asked to document: *"When is this happening or when has it happened slightly already in other classrooms grades, or situations at school or even outside of school?"*

_____

_____

_____

_____

4. **Develop strategies:** The leader asks the student, teachers, parent, and staff members who are present to decide which exceptions can be used and adapted in the classroom and at home for the next few weeks.

Classroom strategies:

_____

_____

Curriculum addition based on exceptions:

_____

_____

Home strategies:

_____

_____

5. **Scaling progress:** The leader restates the rating scores from the beginning of the conversation and asks the participants what rating they hope the student will achieve by the next meeting.

Parent: _____   Student: _____   Teachers: _____

School counselor: _____

Summary: The teacher asks the parent and student, *"What was helpful for you today in this conversation?"*

_____

_____

Next meeting date: _____   Time: _____

Exception Findings: Level B

Date: _____

Student: _____ Grade: _____

The documentation on this page is *only* for exceptions—times, situations, or activities when the student begins to be more successful in the classroom.

Week 1 Exceptions: List activities, situations, assignments:

1. _____

2. _____

3. _____

4. _____

5. _____

Weekly score: _____ Student: _____ Teacher: _____

Week 2 Exceptions: List activities, situations, or assignments:

1. _____

2. _____

3. _____

4. _____

5. _____

Weekly score: _____ Student: _____ Teacher: _____

Week 3 Exceptions: List activities, situations, or assignments:

1. _____

2. _____

3. _____

4. _____

5. _____

Weekly score: _____ Student: _____ Teacher: _____

Exception Observations: Level C

Student: _____ Teacher: _____

Dear Teacher,

There will be a solution-focused RTI Level C meeting for _____

_____ on _____

at _____ in room _____. Your presence is

requested because you are an important member in the student's academic life. The meeting will not last longer than thirty minutes.

Prior to the meeting, please notice times when this student is slightly successful in your classroom. Note the kinds of lessons, activities, behavioral interventions, motivational strategies, or other methods that help the student be slightly more successful. Also note how diet or physician-prescribed medications seem to affect or help the student's learning abilities. Watch for vision and hearing issues, and notice when those issues seem not to interfere with learning. These "exceptions" to times when the student is less successful should be listed below. Please list at least five exceptions below, and bring the list to the meeting.

Thank you.

_____

Exceptions:

1. _____

_____

2. _____

_____

3. _____

_____

4. _____

_____

5. _____

_____

Solution-Focused RTI Conversation: Level C

Date: _____

Student: _____ Grade: _____

Primary teacher: _____ Team: _____

Attendees:

_____

_____

1. **Identify hopes:** The leader opens by expressing appreciation to those attending the meeting, and then starts the conversation: *"What are your best hopes for our meeting today?"*

   (It is common for attendees to answer by saying what they do *not* want. Help those who respond in this way to develop a more workable goal by asking, "What do you want to happen instead?")

   _____

   _____

   _____

   _____

   _____

   "On a scale of 1 to 10, with '1' being not successful and '10' being completely successful, where is the student in regard to what we want to achieve?"

   Parent: _____ Student: _____ Teachers (take average score):

   _____ School counselor: _____

2. **Set goals:** The leader thanks everyone for their responses and asks, *"What will the student be doing in the classroom over the next three weeks so that the score increases and our concern decreases?"*

   _____

   _____

   _____

(continued)

Solution-Focused RTI Conversation: Level C (*Continued*)

3. **Identify exceptions:** The leader asks about the exceptions that everyone present was asked to document: *"When is this happening or when has it happened slightly already, in other classrooms, grades, or situations at school or even outside of school?"*

_____

_____

_____

_____

_____

"I will read some successes that were noted in Level A and Level B. Who has found that one of these strategies has assisted in raising the student's weekly rating score?"

_____

_____

_____

"When else in the past has this student been able to increase academic success on a small scale? Was it in tutoring, in group work, with individual help, or something else?"

_____

_____

"What was different or helpful in that situation?"

_____

_____

4. **Develop strategies:** The leader asks the team and parent (or parents), *"Which additional resources do you think might help the student be more successful?"* (some examples: vision screening, hearing screening, developmental milestone assessment)

_____

_____

_____

_____

To resource personnel: *"When could we get some assessment data from you?"*

_____

The leader asks the student, parent, teachers, and staff members who are present to decide which exceptions can be used and adapted in the classroom and at home for the next few weeks while the community resource personnel conduct assessments.

Classroom strategies:

_____

_____

Curriculum addition based on exceptions:

_____

_____

Home strategies:

_____

_____

Summary: The leader asks the teachers, staff members, resource staff members, parent, and student: *"What was helpful for you today in this conversation?"*

_____

_____

_____

_____

_____

Next meeting date: _____ Time: _____

Exception Findings: Level C

Date: _____

Student: _____ Grade: _____

The documentation on this page is *only* for exceptions—times, situations, or activities when the student begins to be more successful in the classroom.

Week 1 Exceptions: List activities, situations, assignments:

1. _____

2. _____

3. _____

4. _____

5. _____

Weekly score: _____ Student: _____ Teacher: _____

Week 2 Exceptions: List activities, situations, assignments:

1. _____

2. _____

3. _____

4. _____

5. _____

Weekly score: _____ Student: _____ Teacher: _____

Week 3 Exceptions: List activities, situations, assignments:

1. _____

2. _____

3. _____

4. _____

5. _____

Weekly score: _____ Student: _____ Teacher: _____

Solution-Focused Individualized Education Plan (IEP)

Date: _____

Student: _____   Grade: _____

A. Physical Competencies

1. Physical requirements that affect participation in instructional settings:

    _____ No physical limitations; no modification of regular class needed

    _____ Some physical limitations; no modification of regular class needed

    _____ Needs modifications because of the following impairment:

    _____

    In what activities does the impairment *not* affect the student or affect the student less? List specific activities:

    _____

    _____

    Describe the modifications needed, based on the listed activities:

    _____

    _____

2. Physical requirements that affect physical education:

    _____ Yes _____ No The student is capable of receiving instruction in the essential elements of physical education through the regular program without modifications.

    If no, list activities in which the student *is* able to receive instruction:

    _____

    _____

    Recommendation, based on competencies in the listed activities:

    _____

    _____

(continued)

Solution-Focused Individualized Education Plan (IEP) (*continued*)

B. Behavioral Competencies

1. Educational placement and programming:

   _____ Student requires no modifications.

   _____ Student has some characteristics that may affect learning, though not severe enough to withdraw from regular classes:

   _____ Poor task completion

   _____ Impulsive—requires reminding to work slowly

   _____ Other: _____

   Abilities that emerge in specific learning tasks or activities and enhance cooperation in the classroom, as identified by teachers, administrators, or parents:

   _____

   _____

   _____

2. Ability to follow disciplinary rules:

   _____ Appropriate for age and cultural group. May be treated the same as non-handicapped student. Student is able to follow the district's discipline management plan. Use of alternative educational placement and suspension per regulations is appropriate. Student is responsible for school board rules and campus policies without modifications.

   _____ This student is responsible for school board rules and campus procedure. A modified discipline plan will be used. The following approaches have been identified as *effective* in working with this student through direct observation by teachers, administrators, or parents:

   _____

   _____

   _____

C. Pre-Vocational or Vocational Competencies

The following skills may be prerequisite to vocational education. Rate each on a scale of 1 to 10 in which "1" = completely unskilled and "10" = completely competent.

_____ Cognitive skills   _____ Communication skills

_____ Reading level   _____ Organizational skills

_____ Performance   _____ Social skills

_____ Verbal comprehension   _____ Following directions

_____ Attendance   _____ Personal hygiene and self-care

_____ Punctuality

Other: _____

Noting all skills with a rating of 6 or higher, list opportunities within the school program that seem appropriate for a student with those competencies:

_____

_____

_____

_____

_____

D. Academic and Developmental Competencies

1. Rate the student's *competence* in each of the following content areas on a scale of 1 to 10 in which "1" = completely unskilled and "10" = completely competent. (Grade or age levels alone are not sufficient.)

_____ All subjects	_____ English	_____ Health
_____ Reading	_____ Science	_____ Vocational skills
_____ Math	_____ Spelling	_____ Fine arts
_____ Social studies	_____ Computer literacy	_____ Physical education

Other: _____

2. List the subject competencies that are scored 6 or higher below, and in collaboration with the assigned teacher, briefly describe the teaching methods that have been identified as *effective* with this student.

Subject   **Effective Teaching Methods**

_____

_____

_____

_____

_____

_____

(continued)

Solution-Focused Individualized Education Plan (IEP) (*Continued*)

3. Indicate with a checkmark the content areas in which the student needs more assistance in developing competence and could benefit from a special education program.

_____ All subjects   _____ English   _____ Health

_____ Reading   _____ Science   _____ Vocational
                                                                      skills

_____ Math   _____ Spelling   _____ Fine arts

_____ Social   _____ Computer   _____ Physical
                 studies   literacy   education

Other: _____

4. List the checked subjects from item 3 in the space below, and match appropriate teaching methods from item 2 that have been proven effective and that might lead to more competent performance.

Subject   **Suggested Teaching Method**

_____

_____

_____

_____

_____

_____

Source: Adapted from Metcalf, 2008b, p. 113.

504 Conversation for Success

Date: _____

Student: _____ Grade: _____

Attendees:

_____

_____

Primary concern:

_____

Miracle question: Suppose tomorrow when you return to school, things have changed so that you have a good day. What will be different then? Who will do things differently during that day, including you and your teachers?

_____

_____

_____

_____

What difference will that make for you?

_____

_____

_____

Exceptions—Tell me about times when some of your ideas have occurred in the past:

_____

_____

_____

_____

_____

Let's develop some strategies for you and your teachers, based on your ideas:

_____

_____

_____

_____

Student: _____ 504 committee chair: _____

504 Meeting Summary for Teachers—Sample

Date: 5-10-10

Student: Jeremy S.   Grade: 4

Dear Teachers,

Jeremy S. has identified what would help him to be more successful at school. Please talk briefly with the student about his ideas and try out these strategies for the next three weeks with him.

1. It helps me when the teacher asks me whether I understand the assignment before going on to another topic. I am shy, so I don't always ask.
2. If a teacher shows me how to study for a test, I am less anxious and I do better.
3. I do better when I work in a group.
4. I learn best in a quiet area away from friends.
5. I stay on track when another student who knows the assignment works with me.
6. Sometimes I need one extra day to finish an assignment.

Please comment about what seems to be helpful for this student and return this sheet to the 504 committee chair in three weeks.

What's working:

_____

_____

_____

_____

_____

_____

_____

Teacher Signature

Appendix B
Internet Resources

RTI Resources

Center on Teaching and Learning
    http://reading.uoregon.edu/
Intervention Central
    http://www.interventioncentral.org/
Joe Witt—Research and Resources on STEEP and RTI
    http://www.joewitt.org/
Lab for Instructional Consultation Teams
    http://www.icteams.umd.edu/
National Reading Styles Institute
    http://www.nrsi.com/
Scholastic: A Comprehensive Reading Intervention Solution
    http://teacher.scholastic.com/products/read180/
Scientifically Based Research—A Link from Research to Practice
    http://www.gosbr.net/
STEEP—System to Enhance Educational Performance
    http://www.isteep.com/
Using Technology to Support Diverse Learners
    www.w-w-c.org

Other Resources

Academy of Achievement
    achievement.org
Gonzalo Garza Independence High School
    www.austinisd.org/schools/website.phtml?id=024
GreatSchools
    greatschools.net
Happy Dyslexic
    happydyslexic.com

HealthCentral
    healthcentral.com
Institute for Solution-Focused Therapy
    www.solutionfocused.net/solutionfocusedtherapy.html
TEKS (Texas Essential Knowledge and Skills)
    www.tea.state.tx.us/index2.aspx?id=6148
Union County Public Schools
    www.ucps.k12.nc.us/forms_manager/documents/Descriptionof
    TierIII-UCPS.doc

References

Austin Independent School District. (n.d.). Of AISD's 12 high schools, Garza has the highest average SAT scores. Retrieved from http://www.austinisd.org/schools/website.phtml?id=024.

Bradshaw, T. (2003). *Keep it simple.* New York: Pocket Books.

de Shazer, S. (1985). *Keys to solution in brief therapy.* New York: Norton .

Education Service Center, Region 20. (2007). *Response to Intervention (RtI): Overview and considerations.* San Antonio, TX: Author.

Glasser, W. (1998). *The quality school.* New York: Harper.

Lauren, J. (1997). *Succeeding with LD: 20 true stories about people with LD.* Minneapolis: Free Spirit.

Metcalf, L. (2008a). *Counseling toward solutions.* Hoboken, NJ: John Wiley. (Original work published 1995.)

Metcalf, L. (2008b). *A field guide to counseling toward solutions: The solution focused school.* Hoboken, NJ: John Wiley.

O'Hanlon, W., & Weiner-Davis, M. (1989). *In search of solutions.* New York: Norton.

Swanson, C. (2008). *Special education in America: The state of students with disabilities in the nation's high schools.* Bethesda, MD: Editorial Projects in Education.

White, M., & Epston, D. (1990). *Narrative means to therapeutic ends.* New York: Norton.

Index

Separation anxiety, examples of, in intermediate school, 120–123

SIT meetings, 108

Social support mechanism, 130

Solution-focused RTI approach: applications of, 27–28; beginning the, suggestions for, 31–34; defining the process of, 10–11; and diverse populations, 18–19; at a glance, *35, 155*; guidelines for, 29–45; implementation of the, staying focused on, assisting with, 150; intention of the, xviii, xix, 49; introducing, in high school, 136, 137, 139; letting students in on the, 123; making the choice of the, 49–50; possibilities for intervention in the, 19; practice of, core ideas in the, 34, 36–45; proven results from the, 157; reflection in, role of, 132–133; and the role of the family, 123; source of the, xviii; and traditional RTI core assumptions, 136–137; as the way to a mind-set change, 141–142. *See also specific aspects of a solution-focused RTI approach*

"Solution-Focused RTI at a Glance" form, *35,* 150, *152, 155*

"Solution-Focused RTI Conversation: Level A" form, *65–66, 67, 155*

"Solution-Focused RTI Conversation: Level B" form, 71, *73–74*

"Solution-Focused RTI Conversation: Level C" form, 86, *87–89*

Speakers, parents as, integration of, 26

Special education: accelerated number of students placed in, issue with, 148; cost of, as an issue, xvii; decrease in referrals for, xix, 21, 27, 64, 157; diverse populations represented in, 18; eligibility for placement in, full evaluation of, obtaining consent for, 83; referring for, following RTI, 34, 77, 90, 92, 110; rushing into testing for, problem of, 141

Special education students: achievement by, 6; number of, national average for, 19

Spielberg, S., 16

State board of education, investigation by the, 148

Steps That Create a Solution-Focused Direction guide, 50–55

Strategies: addressing, in RTI meetings, 33; identifying, in 504 meetings, 56, *58, 59;* unique, discovering, 16–18

Strategies, developing: in Level A conversations, *66;* in Level B conversations, *74;* in Level C conversations, *88–89*

Strengths and abilities: focusing on, 42–43, 135; identifying, 102

Student empowerment, 23, 25, 67, 86, 92, 147

Student Intervention Team (SIT), 108, 114

Student self-awareness, power of, 76

"Student Survey" form, 102, *104*

Student worldviews: cooperating with, 40–41; stepping into, example of, 125

Students, including: beginning with, 31; buy-in resulting from, 50, 53; in defining the goal, 37–38; by helping them to notice changes, 44–45; importance of, 21, 22, 23, 23–25, 26, 142; initially holding off on, 84; systemically, result of, 77. *See also* Team approach

Swanson, C., 18

Switzer, S., 99

Symptoms, seeing past, 40

Systemic perspective, 22–23

T

Target setting, *66*

Targeted instructional interventions. *See* Tier II

Task setting, short-term, engaging in conversation about, *52, 55, 154*

Teachers: follow-up meetings with, 150; introducing solution-focused RTI to, 136, 137, 139; most difficult stage for, 140–141; perceptions of, power of, to influence student behavior, 141; perspectives of, 12, 19, 28, 45; as students' guide to the future, 137

Team approach: creating a, to turn chaos into compliments, 8–10; to developing and delivering strategies, 33; to identifying exceptions, 34; in Level B conversations, 71–79; to reviewing the RTI program, 33; in a solution-focused approach, xviii, xix, 17, 24. *See also* Parents, including; Students, including

Team collaboration, 26, 31

Texas Assessment of Knowledge and Skills (TAKS), 119

Texas Essential Knowledge and Skills (TEKS), 184

Tier I: in action, elementary examples of, 104–106, *107;* aspects of, 3–45; beginning of, experiences leading to, 100–101; brief and effective interventions in, 127–128; continuing support from, 109; as the data-collecting phase, during high school, 140–142; documentation of interventions for, *111;* in the elementary school, described, 101–102; how solution-focused RTI meets the objective of, *35;* and individual attention, 145; materials for, looking at, and changing, 142; moving a student from, 144; overview of, 1; referrals in, during intermediate school, 119; and the RTI continuum, 108; the school counselor and, 120; student survey for, *103*

Tier II: in action, elementary examples of, 108–110; aspects of, 49–79; counseling interventions in, during intermediate school, 129–131; documentation of interventions for, *112;* in the elementary school, described, 106, 108; how solution-focused RTI meets the objective of, *35;* and individual attention, 145; moving a student from, 144–145; moving a student to, 144; overview of, 47; and parental contact, 144;

recommending a student for, example of, 109, 114; and the RTI continuum, 108; unlocking opportunity in, during high school, 142–143

Tier III: in action, elementary examples of, 110, 114; aspects of, 83–156; documentation of interventions for, *113*; in the elementary school, described, 110; as a form of differentiated instruction, 145; how solution-focused RTI meets the objective of, *35*; interventions for, during intermediate school, 131–132; moving a student to, 144–145; overview of, 81; recommending a student for, example of, 114; referring to, 71; and the RTI continuum, 108

Tiers: meeting objectives of the, at a glance, *35*; moving between, 108, 110; using fluid boundaries between, 128

Transition years, 118–119

U

Ultimate tool, 118

Union County Public Schools, 83, 184

Unique strategies, discovering, importance of, 16–18

Using Technology to Support Diverse Learners, 183

V

Vaughn, V., 13

Vega, H., 64

Vision screening, *35*, 83, 84, *88*, 90

Vocational competencies, assessing, *94–95*

W

Wagley, J., 38

Weiner-Davis, M., 34

White, M., 36, 40

Whites, representation of, in special education, 18

Wikipedia, xvii

Winkler, H., 13